CLIMATE IS JUST THE START

CLIMATE IS JUST THE START

MIKAELA LOACH

BRIGHT
MATTER
BOOKS

Text copyright © 2025 by Mikaela Loach
Jacket art copyright © 2025 by Philip Pascuzzo
Interior art copyright © 2025 by Lauri Johnston

All rights reserved. Published in the United States by Bright Matter Books, an imprint
of Random House Children's Books, a division of Penguin Random House LLC,
1745 Broadway, New York, NY 10019.

Bright Matter Books and colophon are registered trademarks of Penguin Random House LLC.

Visit us on the Web! rhcbooks.com

penguinrandomhouse.com

Educators and librarians, for a variety of teaching tools, visit us at RHTeachersLibrarians.com

Library of Congress Cataloging-in-Publication Data is available upon request.
ISBN 978-0-593-89732-4 (trade)—ISBN 978-0-593-89734-8 (lib. bdg.)—
ISBN 978-0-593-89733-1 (ebook)

The text of this book is set in 11.5-point Adobe Garamond Pro.

Printed in the United States of America
10 9 8 7 6 5 4 3 2 1
First Edition

The authorized representative in the EU for product safety and compliance is Penguin
Random House Ireland, Morrison Chambers, 32 Nassau Street, Dublin D02 YH68,
Ireland, https://eu-contact.penguin.ie

For the kids of the Niger Delta, of the Yukpa and Wayuu Indigenous communities, of Tuvalu, of the Amazon, and of every community fighting extractivism and the climate crisis: We will join your fight, and we will make a better world for us all.

I believe that we will win.

CONTENTS

CLIMATE IS JUST THE START

YOU CAN'T CHANGE THE WORLD WITHOUT YOUR FEELINGS

This is a book about our climate.

But maybe you guessed from the title that it's about some other things too.

This is also a book about how our climate—our climate crisis—hurts some people far more than other people, and how unfair that is.

This is also a book about hope!

About how we can actually fix things. About how the solutions are in plain sight, right in front of us.

We can—quite literally—change the world. But before we can change the world, we have to *feel* the world.

And you're in luck. Chances are if you're reading this book

you are young. And when you are young, you are more likely to still have one very important gift—your big feelings. You're going to need those.

That's because you can't change the world without your feelings.

Have you ever looked at a situation you thought was unfair and said to yourself, "That just doesn't make sense!"

It could be something close to home, like in your family or your school.

Or it could be something much farther away. Maybe it's the fact that some of our fellow humans have no safe place to live. Or that billions of people around the world don't have access to enough food or safe drinking water. Perhaps you saw a politician on TV say that they care about the climate crisis and then turn around and create rules and laws that make things worse.

Maybe these situations have made you feel really sad. I know I still cry regularly when I hear news about our climate crisis, read stories about injustice, or learn about a tragedy on social media. My heart breaks often.

When asking questions about things that don't make sense in our world, has anyone ever told you, "Look, it's just the way the world is," or "That's something you'll understand when you're older."

I was a kid who asked lots of questions, and adults would answer me like this. I asked "But why?" a lot, and I was rarely satisfied with the response. I couldn't help wondering: Why is this "just the way that the world is"? Honestly, *why?* Why don't we change the world so that this *isn't* the way it is? Aren't *we* "society," so if together we want the world to change, isn't it up to all of us to do something?

But lots of adults wouldn't want to get into it. And something seemed different about them. They cried less than I did—and, sure, sometimes for understandable reasons—but they also *felt* less. And that was celebrated like it was a *good* thing . . . like it was better to not feel things deeply, to not cry or be moved by injustice, but instead to look through or past it. This made no sense to me. It still doesn't.

If someone is so "tough" that they never cry about anything, this is seen as strength. If someone can witness or experience something sad, scary, or tragic and seem untroubled by it, this is somehow rewarded as bravery.

I see it differently.

I think it's braver to feel heartbreak, even if it hurts. If we completely shut down the part of ourselves that feels bad things, if we toughen ourselves up so much that nothing can reach our hearts, won't it just become easier to ignore the bad things, like how much pain there is in our world? To just let it pass? And who wins if we do that?

I believe the correct response—the natural human response—is to react to unfairness and harm in our world with a broken heart. This softness is a *strength*. A power. It is absolutely not a weakness. To *not* be moved? That is what is unnatural.

If you are not moved by the world, you will not act to move the world. It's that simple.

So hold on to your soft heart. It's the most important thing you can do! The world needs your soft heart. Allow it to

XIII

break—but please don't stay stuck in the heartbreak. Feel all the feelings, but don't let them overcome you. Channel them. Find a way to transform them into something else. This book will help you learn how we can do this.

Let's find a way to make what moves us move the world. Together.

PART 1

1

THE STORY OF THE DISAPPEARING BEACHES

It's probably time for me to introduce myself, right?

Hi, my name is Mikaela! I'm a climate justice activist, and I live in a seaside city in England. Growing up, I had no clue what a climate justice activist was, but I had a sense of what the word *justice* meant. I knew when I saw something unfair, either close to my home or in the wider world. And I cared about making those unfair things fair. Like many of us, I wanted to make the world a better place.

Lots of this came from understanding that as a Black woman in the United Kingdom and as a descendant of enslaved people, so many who came before me had fought for the freedoms I had and built the world I lived in.

I grew up feeling a little guilty that I got to live a reasonably

safe and free life while so many people who came before me died fighting for this. I wanted to honor their sacrifices. I wanted to do the best I could with the freedoms and privileges I had been given. Maybe this is a feeling you've had too.

I'd talk to anyone who would listen about issues that had caught my heart's attention. I'd give talks in school assemblies about the importance of donating blood, the harm and inequality women experience all over the world, the impact of our diets on animals and the climate crisis, and much, much more.

I'd organize friends to volunteer with me to chop wood, fold clothes, and cook food to support displaced people— sometimes called *refugees*—on the France–UK border. And in the background, I was studying to become a doctor.

I was told over and over that if I wanted to help people and I was good at school, being a doctor was the best way to go. Since I didn't grow up around "activists," becoming a doctor seemed like the only real chance I had to "make a difference."

In school, concepts like *human rights* and *oppression* were often presented as a kind of "done deal." Like, "Oh, a long time ago people fought and won, so now we are all set." Rather than continuing to learn about and fight injustice, we were told to be grateful we were now free. So I studied as hard as I could and got into medical school. I wanted to work on search-and-rescue ships in the Mediterranean Sea, to help prevent the drowning of refugees as they make their journey to Europe in small boats.

But when I got to medical school, something changed in me. I began to feel deeply aware of the huge impact of the climate crisis. I grew afraid for my future, and about the present-day conditions for billions of people across the world.

So I started turning my fear into action. I started meeting people—activists—who felt the same way I did, and we began working together. We organized rallies and occupations of government buildings; we challenged powerful oil companies and politicians; we planned campaigns to call out governments that weren't doing enough; we used social media to raise awareness and bring more people on board; and we even took the UK government to court. It was in these spaces that my understanding of climate justice grew.

It felt so exciting. I could see the power we all have to change things. It was like if you don't know you need glasses, and then you try on your friend's pair and can see so much clearer and farther than before. **I could *see* a better future, I could *feel* it, and I believed that we could build it.** It changed the entire direction of my life.

Climate justice is an idea we will explore deeply in this book. For now, though, all you need to understand is something I

learned when I was younger: We can't just keep sticking a Band-Aid on the wounds of this world. Maybe a Band-Aid will stop the bleeding for a bit, but the wounds are deep and wide. We must treat them and heal them, rather than just patching them up.

But how do we do that? How do we heal our wounds instead of slapping a Band-Aid on them? How do we confront the climate crisis *and* make a world where no one has to risk drowning in the sea while journeying to find a safe home? That is what this book is about. That is what we will explore together. And the first step is working out how—and why—the world has these wounds in the first place.

How do we heal our wounds instead of slapping a Band-Aid on them?

MY DISAPPEARING BEACH

I was born on a small island called Jamaica.

You've probably sung the lyric "Every little thing is gonna be all right" by the famous Jamaican musician Bob Marley. Or perhaps you've seen our athletes—some of the fastest people in the world—win gold medals at the Olympic Games. You might be Jamaican yourself, or you might have vacationed on the white sandy beaches and warm seas there. For such a small island, the impact we have had on the world is huge. But this same island might not be around forever.

When I was a child, my parents and grandparents often took me to Hellshire Beach. I remember running around on the sand, swimming in the crystal clear sea, laughing a lot with my grandma and my cousins, and eating fried plantains and festivals (pieces of fried dough) in the colorful restaurants that sit on stilts. When we moved from Jamaica to the UK, it was these memories of Hellshire Beach that helped connect me to my homeland. **They kept me warm in the colder climate where I was raised.**

Years later, during the COVID-19 pandemic, when we all had to stay home to keep each other safe, I decided to move back to my birth island to reconnect with my heritage and my family. My granddad in Jamaica had recently passed away, and I was grieving the time I'd lost with him. And I wanted to deepen my relationship with my wonderful and hilarious grandma.

As soon as I landed in Jamaica and settled into my new home overlooking the turquoise sea, I called Grandma on Face-Time. I told her how excited I was to see her and to return to Hellshire together.

Her face fell into sadness. "Mikaela," she said, "that beach has almost disappeared."

My stomach sank. How could this be true?

I was devastated with what I found. Where there had once been an expanse of sand, the water was lapping ever closer to the restaurants on stilts. **My memories and my connection to my birthland were being washed away too.**

My grandmother lives only about a ten-minute drive from Hellshire. And many communities live right on the shore. I started to wonder: How much longer will she be safe? At this point, I had been a climate justice campaigner for many years, so I understood the gravity of Hellshire's disappearance.

Maybe you've heard similar stories: **of beaches eroding, of hurricanes becoming more powerful, or of sea levels getting higher.** If you haven't, that's okay. Let's get into it together!

So what's happening?

The world is getting hotter. And when temperatures increase over time, more water than usual evaporates from rivers, seas, lakes, and oceans. The extra water ends up in the atmosphere in the form of gas. This gas in turn traps heat in the air, increasing temperatures even more.

When warmer, water-filled air meets colder air, the water becomes liquid again and falls as heavy rain or storms. In some parts of the world, this isn't a big problem yet. But in tropical areas like the Caribbean—where Jamaica is situated—when these storms are really big and have very strong winds, we refer to them as *hurricanes.* Hurricanes are so powerful that they can rip up the earth, topple trees, and destroy buildings. They are super-dangerous, putting people's lives and homes at risk.

Climate change is making powerful storms happen more often and with greater intensity. It was hurricanes that damaged the shores of Hellshire Beach. They have overwhelmed humanmade and

> **Climate change is making powerful storms happen more often and with greater intensity.**

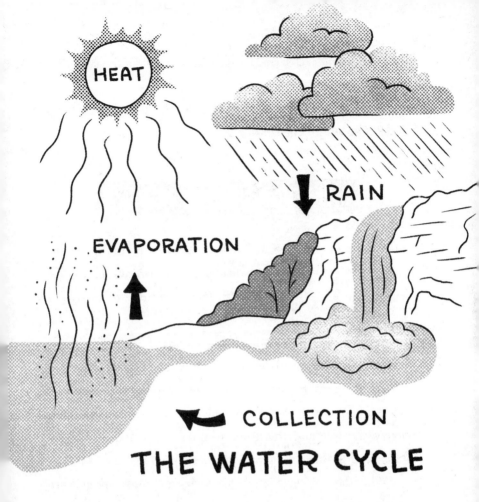

THE WATER CYCLE

natural defenses, like stone barriers and vegetation. These defenses don't work as they should anymore and can no longer keep the water from erasing our beach.

To make things harder, global sea levels are rising at the same time temperatures are. When gigantic icebergs and glaciers melt, all that extra water pours right into the sea. And when too much ice melts too quickly, all that extra water flows onto our islands, covering people's homes and all the land they exist on.

This isn't some idea about the far-out future: It's happening today. And not just in Jamaica.

MY FRIEND'S DISAPPEARING BEACH

I have a friend named Kato Ewekia, who lives in Tuvalu, a small island nation in the South Pacific. An alarming amount of Tuvalu has already disappeared underwater due to rising sea levels.

When Kato was growing up, like me with Hellshire, he had a favorite beach. It was covered with soft sand, perfect for a game of tag, racing his friends, or a game called Funny (which he told me is a variation of tag, but where there are two teams—one tagging people and the other stacking cans to spell *funny*). This beach brought Kato and his friends so much joy.

When he was eight years old, his parents took him and his brother to Fiji for three years. When they returned home to Tuvalu, eleven-year-old Kato, now into rugby, asked his friends if they could all go play on the beach again. One friend said to him, "Kato, that beach is gone." In the short time he'd been away, a big tropical storm had stolen it from the people of Tuvalu.

Kato looked for somewhere else they could play rugby, but the only beach he could find now was covered with rocks that hurt them when they fell. He kept searching for a sandier one, but they had all been submerged by water. So they learned to play on the rocky beach. They learned to deal with the pain the rocks left on their bodies.

Kato then left for Fiji with his parents for another three years. When he returned, even the rocky beach was gone! The sea was moving farther and farther in, claiming more and more of his memories, his favorite places, and his ability to play and have fun with his friends. Since rugby wasn't possible anymore, he thought he would spend his free time fishing instead—that with all that water, fishing would be okay. Kato's uncle was a fisherman, and Kato loved spending time on the ocean with him.

But, just like it ruined rugby, the climate crisis ruined fishing for him too.

In the same way surface and air temperatures have increased due to the climate crisis, water temperatures have too. The sea is now much warmer than it should be. On fishing trips, Kato noticed they were having to go out farther and farther to deeper and deeper waters, because the fish had moved to find cooler waters. Fishing was an essential food source for Tuvalu, but now when Tuvaluan fishermen would go fishing for tuna, they would have to go so far that they couldn't even see the islands anymore.

This made these trips far scarier, since the risk of getting caught in more dangerous waters was higher, and finding their way back to the island was far more difficult. Some of Kato's friends disappeared while fishing. Some were finally found, but far too many didn't make it home and were never seen again. Like the beaches, they were swallowed by the warming, growing ocean. **Their lives were stolen by the climate crisis.**

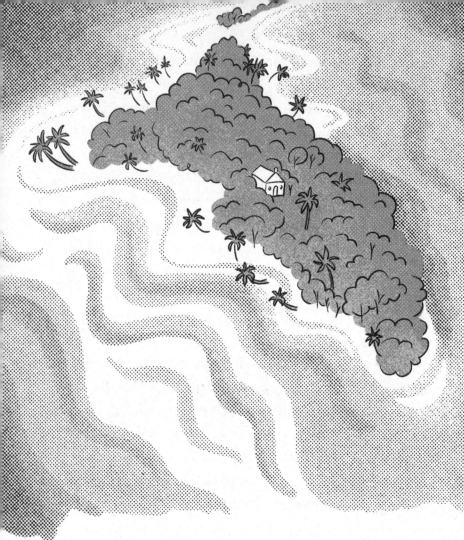

Sea-level rise was impacting every aspect of Tuvalu. It wasn't just that places to play and find joy were being taken away. It wasn't just that the ability to fish for food was becoming more difficult. The ability to *grow* food was disappearing.

As the sea level kept increasing, the amount of salt in the soil became too high. It used to be that once a year there would be a very high tide, referred to as a *king's tide*. This high tide could cause flooding and damage to crops. But now, Kato says, "Every high tide is like a king's tide." Because of this, it's become impossible for Tuvaluans to depend on crops for food. So now they have to depend on imported food from grocery stores.

This food is unhealthy and extremely expensive. **Because Tuvalu is so remote, it's hard to ship products from overseas.** Most food that makes it there has spent months in freezer containers in ships coming from Australia and Fiji; it's not fresh at all by the time it arrives. And as lots of this food is preserved and highly processed, it causes dangerous health conditions like diabetes and high blood pressure. But Kato says that they have "no choice," that "it's the only food to survive on."

You might already be thinking that this is shocking. But I was even more taken aback when Kato told me about a very strong tropical storm in 2015, known as Cyclone Pam. The whipping winds and waves generated by the massive cyclone were more than Tuvalu could take. The effect on people living there was immense: Almost half the population was displaced from their homes. Remaining essential food sources—from crops to livestock—were killed, and drinking water was contaminated.

And it wasn't just the living who were impacted. "The waves brought all the bones of our ancestors out from the ground," Kato told me, explaining how horrifying it was. "They were put there to rest their souls, and the waves brought them up and took their headstones." Even Tuvalu's dead were not safe from the climate crisis.

Since Cyclone Pam, Kato has been afraid, he says, and "living day by day hoping that home does not disappear." He has no idea how much longer home will be there.

But Kato does not let fear control him. In the face of all of this loss, he refuses to give up.

Through social media, he saw young people like himself all over the world taking to the streets, striking from school, calling out big companies, and demanding real climate action. He didn't know much about activism, but he did know he wanted to save his home. Scientists were predicting Tuvalu would be *gone* in ten to fifteen years if adequate climate action was not taken.

After appearing in a documentary about the impacts of sea-level rise, Kato connected with young people in Mexico who had started a climate justice campaign called Saving Tuvalu. Kato was worried his English wasn't good enough, but he joined the group anyway.

This crucial step took him to the United Nations Climate Change Conference in Glasgow, Scotland—more commonly known as COP26—in 2021. He was the first Tuvaluan youth to attend a UN climate conference, and that's where he and I first met. Since then, Kato has traveled across the world to raise awareness of the impacts of the climate crisis on Tuvalu.

Back at home, he has inspired other young Tuvaluans to get involved, through a group called Climate Mobility Tuvalu. At first, some young people were hesitant. In their culture, there is a lot of respect for elders, and many young people believed that taking action would be disrespectful to older people, who historically were called upon to fix big problems.

"Youth all over the world are leading!" Kato would tell them. "Doing climate activism is to help the community. Sometimes our elders can't do everything . . . **If we are doing something for the betterment of the future, our ancestors would be proud, because we have their backs.**"

Thanks to his hard work, Kato was no longer the only Tuvaluan youth activist at the UN climate conference two years later, at COP28 in Dubai. Alongside other young Pacific Islanders, they chanted, "We are not drowning. We are rising."

2

FOSSILS ARE FUELING IT

It is shocking that Kato's home could disappear underwater in just a few years, right? It is worrying. It is urgent. But to do something to stop it, we have to understand *why* it's happening.

By now you're probably wondering, "What's causing all of this"? You understand that rising global temperatures are melting glaciers and ice caps, disrupting the water cycle, raising sea levels, and increasing the frequency and intensity of extreme weather events. But *why* are global temperatures rising?

These global temperature increases—and how frequent and ferocious hurricanes, wildfires, droughts, and floods are getting—are *not natural*. While Earth does have natural cycles of cooler and warmer temperatures, the dramatic increases we are experiencing are *contrary to where we should be in these natural cycles.*

So what's causing this?

We'll have to go back in time to work this out. Which means we're going to hop into Mikaela's Time Machine! It's pink, my favorite color (fun fact: I pretty much only wear pink clothes), and it's powered by feelings of curiosity, passion, and imagination. We're going to do this a lot throughout the book, so buckle up!

Okay, I'm setting the controls to the year 1960. Why 1960? That might seem kind of random.

But it's not. Around 1960, Earth's surface temperatures are starting to increase outside of natural cycles. Why the change? Well, what else is increasing at the same time?

In 1960, we have the formation of the Beatles, we have some great style, we have a lot of people fighting for civil rights in the United States, and . . . we've started buying and using way more stuff. **When we buy and use things, that's called *consumption*.** And more consumption means more factories to make the things we buy, and more ships and airplanes to transport them to us.

From the 1960s onward, consumption in the US, the UK, Canada, Australia, countries in Europe, and other richer nations began to increase ever more dramatically. Air travel steadily grew, as did individual car ownership and reliance on imported goods. Soon came lots of electrical devices—air-conditioning, computers, and cell phones—which all required energy to make them work. So consumption is a *huge* factor driving the climate crisis. We'll be coming back to this later.

Lurking behind all of this consumption, all of the transportation and the energy used for electrical goods, *and* all production is one thing. **What's this thing?**

Fossil fuels.

We'll be going into some depth about fossil fuel companies later on, but for now there are some important things to understand.

Fossil fuels are fossils that are used as fuel. Pretty simple, right? They are made from organic matter—from animals, trees, and other plants that died thousands of years ago. Over time, their remains were pressed down by the earth until the carbon in them condensed in the form of coal, oil, or gas. These substances—oil, gas, and coal—are full of carbon and energy.

Burning fossil fuels releases this energy. It powers ships, airplanes, cars, stoves, heaters, machines, and so much more. Unfortunately, it doesn't produce just energy. When a fossil fuel is burned, the carbon from the fuel bonds with oxygen already in the air to form another gas: carbon dioxide.

Carbon dioxide is called a *greenhouse gas.* This is because it has special properties for holding in heat—making Earth and our atmosphere like a greenhouse. Maybe you've been in a greenhouse yourself—my Nana in the UK had one. The greenhouse would keep in heat, creating the warm environment needed for her tomatoes to grow. Basically, greenhouses trap in heat.

In a similar way, carbon dioxide (CO_2 for short) traps in heat. So when there is too much CO_2, the temperature of the atmosphere increases.

In other words, more CO_2 in the atmosphere means more

heat is trapped in the atmosphere. This process is referred to as *the greenhouse effect*. But unlike the greenhouse in my Nana's garden, this greenhouse isn't helping tomatoes to ripen. This greenhouse is covering the whole world. **It's making many parts of Earth unbearable places to live**—and causing many of the problems we have already discussed and more.

So: Burning fossil fuels releases carbon dioxide, which traps more heat in the atmosphere, which increases temperatures at ground level, heats oceans, melts glaciers, and dangerously shifts weather patterns.

Because of burning fossil fuels, Kato has already lost his favorite beaches and one whole island near his home, and Tuvaluans are finding it almost impossible to grow food and catch fish. *Continuing* to burn fossil fuels would drown the whole of Tuvalu under rising seas.

Expert scientists have warned us again and again: If we all want a future we can live in, we cannot have *any* new oil, gas, or coal.

But governments around the world—including the UK, the US, Norway, Australia, and the United Arab Emirates—are ignoring this. **They are still allowing fossil fuel companies** to extract *millions* of barrels of oil—and plan to for decades to come. These governments and companies know that burning fossil fuels will kill billions of people. And yet it continues.

Why?

If we all want a future we can live in, we cannot have *any* new oil, gas, or coal.

It's because some people want more money for themselves and do not care if the rest of us live or die. That might be a difficult thing to hear. Maybe it feels to you like one of those situations that "just doesn't make sense." And you're right—it doesn't. But the people in charge of fossil fuel companies have proven over and over again that they don't care about anyone but themselves, no matter what their fancy advertisements might say.

Did you know that, according to a 2019 report, just twenty companies are responsible for more than a third of all carbon emissions in the modern era? Can you guess what all these companies have in common?

Every single one of them is a fossil fuel company. Chevron, Shell, Saudi Aramco, BP (formally known as British Petroleum), ExxonMobil, and fifteen more fossil fuel companies alone are responsible for 35 percent of those emissions worldwide. **And they've been making billions of dollars the whole time.**

You probably have a lot of questions, and the biggest one might be: "Why hasn't our government stopped the burning of fossil fuels if we know they are causing this crisis?"

It has something to do with the companies that are making lots of money from them.

We will be answering so many of these questions, but, in the meantime, take a moment and think about how all of this makes you feel. **How did Kato's story make you feel?** How does understanding that burning fossil fuels has caused this crisis make you feel?

Sometimes I feel overwhelmed. You might feel overwhelmed

too. You are young, and you are new on this planet, and now you have to save it from being destroyed? Sounds super-unfair and kind of intense, doesn't it?

WE ARE THE GENERATION THAT GETS TO CHANGE EVERYTHING

Guess what? It *is* super-unfair, and it *is* intense. But we don't get to check out! And that's not actually a bad thing. We are the generation who gets to change *everything*. The climate crisis is exposing how unfair this world is, but *we have the chance to make it fair*. We have the chance to make it better. We have the chance to pull out the rotted roots that have grown a rotten world for so many people. A world that allows a handful of people to steal valuable resources from everyone else.

Our world, the world we build together, can be one where **no one has to live without food or a safe home or clean water.** A world where no one experiences harm because they are not considered important enough. A world where we all get to live with dignity. Sounds pretty great, right? Well, it's within our reach! We just have to fight for it. It's the most important and exciting fight humanity has ever faced. And we get to do this together. Are you ready to join us?

3

CLIMATE IS JUST THE START

In the beginning of this book, we talked about the importance of having a soft heart and the bravery of allowing yourself to feel heartbreak. In addition to letting our hearts break, we have to also find what can mend them.

To start repairing a broken heart, you need a vision of the future that is so wonderful—so exciting—that it makes your heart beat faster, a vision that you can't help but do everything you can to move toward.

For me, that vision is climate justice.

Where have you heard the term *climate justice*? Maybe you've seen it written on a poster or a placard at a protest, or in a post on social media. Maybe you've talked about it at school. Or maybe you'd never heard of it before you started reading this book. I was much older than you when I first found out about climate justice. But when I did, it changed my whole life!

Before I understood climate justice, I saw the climate crisis as an issue for privileged people who didn't have more urgent things to worry about. As a kid, I saw that there were billions of people struggling to survive in this world. I saw that there were Black people being killed by the police. I saw millions of people across the world without a safe home to live in or enough food to eat, and families torn apart by racist border systems. These were the issues I wanted to tackle! Also, simply "protecting the environment" while at the same time maintaining an unequal world for the people *in* that environment wasn't exciting to me. Instead, it frustrated me!

Climate justice showed me that "preserving" the world isn't enough. Preserving the world means keeping things the way they are. What really thrills me isn't the idea of preservation; it's the idea of transformation.

You might have already guessed that climate justice has something to do with both the climate crisis and justice. But what sort of justice? *Justice* can mean a lot of

> **What really thrills me isn't the idea of preservation; it's the idea of transformation.**

different things to a lot of people. For some, it brings up images of courtrooms, lawyers, and judges. For others, maybe it's superheroes fighting villains. The *justice* in *climate justice* has two sides.

THE FIRST SIDE OF "JUSTICE"

The first side involves social *in*justice—the unfairness in the way the climate crisis impacts different people, and how this unfairness plays out in other areas of the world as well.

It's important to understand that not all people are equally impacted by the climate crisis. **We might all be in the same storm**—in the sense that we are all impacted or will be impacted by the climate crisis in some way—**but we are *not* all in the same boat.** Some of us are in huge, strong ships that can withstand the storm more safely and easily, and others are in small, rickety rafts that are far more likely to be destroyed by the same storm.

When someone has an advantage over someone else, like this one—a stronger boat that leaves some safe and others in

danger—**that is a kind of unfairness called *inequity*.** And our world is full of inequity. So many of our fellow humans are stuck in the same storm with leaky boats, all too ready to sink.

So that's the "what" of climate justice: the fact that some of us are much more affected by the climate crisis due to inequity.

We also need to understand the "why." Why do some people experience the terrible effects of the climate crisis while others don't as much? The answer to that question is a lot deeper, and we are going to get into it! But for now, the simplest answer is: It has to do with power.

Power works in a lot of ways. Some are obvious; others are trickier. Some you can see; others you can't. Flip a light switch, and your room is suddenly brighter. Watch a wave crash around you, and suddenly you feel yourself swept along. These are physical forms of power. They generate real force, and we can see and feel them.

Other forms of power are invisible, but they generate just as much force and help dictate how we live. Where does this kind of power come from? Lots of places. It can come from ideas, or beliefs, or stories that lots of people choose to believe. When we create rules or practices based on these ideas, beliefs, or stories, we create something called a *system of power.* One example of this is racism. You can't see or touch racism, but it has real power in impacting people's lives.

We are going to talk more about systems of power, but for now let's get back to those leaky boats. It's not an accident that so many are stuck in these unsafe boats while fewer get to enjoy the safe boats. It's not that those in the safe boats are inherently better or stronger than those forced into the weak boats. In fact, the safe boats are so big and so strong only because they have stripped the other boats of their materials and resources. They make the small boats even smaller and weaker in order to strengthen and grow themselves.

But how can this be? **How did people end up in different classes of boats?** Well, the truth is that in our world some people are considered more important, and others are considered not as important. This is an example of something called a *hierarchy*.

A hierarchy is a way of ranking people (or groups of people) above or below other people. These rankings are based on opinions of what people are worth or how much they matter.

If you're saying, "What is she talking about?" think back to your last field day at school or a race at the Olympic Games. Remember whatever your favorite event was—perhaps it was the egg-and-spoon relay or the 100-meter sprint or the three-legged race. At the end of the competition, those who finish first, second, and third sometimes get to stand on a podium. At least, that's what happens in the medal ceremonies at the Olympic Games. The person who wins is on a podium higher than the others, the person who comes in second is a bit lower than first, and the person who comes in third is even lower. The person who comes in first also gets the biggest and shiniest medal—in the Olympic Games, they get a gold one. And the value of the medal goes down as the positions get lower—from gold to silver to bronze.

Hierarchies are like this, but also not like this. While in

a race, people earn their medals by being fast, lots of hierarchies determine who goes where by choosing who looks the fastest, rather than who actually is. They rank people, position people, and reward people differently, but not based on performance—instead, based on ideas of what is the best, what is the most valuable, and often, **who gets to be the *most* human.** And rather than different medals, people end up with different living standards: better or worse homes, more or less food, more or less free time, more safety or more vulnerability to climate disasters. Remember how we talked about invisible systems of power a little while ago? A hierarchy like this one is a big example!

Does this seem a bit overwhelming? It's pretty horrible that the world is structured in a way that is unfair. It might make you feel a bit low, and maybe even a bit doomy, but remember—I said there were two sides to this. Now we get to the exciting part!

THE SECOND SIDE OF "JUSTICE"

The *other* side to the *justice* in *climate justice* is this: Because the climate crisis is so fundamentally connected to our world's unfairness, **to fight the climate crisis is to also fight that unfairness.**

So in tackling the climate crisis, the best we can hope for is not just stopping complete climate breakdown. The best we can hope for is a *transformed, free,* and *joy-filled world*!

By making visible the existing connections between the systems causing the climate crisis and the systems that have manufactured other crises for so many decades, climate justice offers us a real opportunity to create a fair world. It is the best opportunity we have ever had. We can't waste it!

WHAT CAN YOU DO ABOUT IT?

How do we not waste this opportunity? How do we move the world around us?

For me, it has been a journey. It took me a long time to work out how to turn "feeling moved" into "moving the world." Feeling the things came easily. Moving the things? That wasn't so simple.

That began to change when I was six years old. I remember so clearly that I had snuck downstairs past my bedtime and peeked into the living room. My parents were watching the news, and it was showing video of the massive destruction caused by a tsunami—a huge wave resulting from an earthquake under the ocean—which had devastated vast areas of Sri Lanka and Indonesia.

On the TV, I saw kids, just like me, who had lost their homes or family members, and tears began to stream from my eyes. It all felt so unfair: Why were these kids suffering while I got to be safe and secure? What was the difference between me and them? Wasn't it random that my family and I didn't live there?

I must have made a sound, because my parents realized I

was there at the door. Their faces, filled with concern, matched my glistening cheeks. I joined them on the sofa, and we talked about how I felt.

After comforting me and checking that I was okay, my dad asked me the question that would determine the path of my life from then on: **"Mikaela, if you care about this issue, what are you going to do about it?"**

My dad made it clear that I didn't have to—and couldn't—fix everything, but he also said that didn't mean I couldn't do anything at all. In that moment, I understood that you don't have to be a perfect hero to take action. Whatever we can do matters. If we can save one person, make one life a bit better or a bit safer—it matters. How could that not matter?

So when I started school, I organized a bake sale with some other students. Maybe you've done one of these too. I made my first batch of straw-

If we can save one person, make one life a bit better or a bit safer—it matters.

berry cupcakes with my mom, decorating them with icing, sprinkles, and colorful paper wafers. Classmates contributed

brownies, chocolate-cornflake cakes, and flapjacks. Our bake sale wasn't big, but by working together, we raised much more money than I would have been able to raise on my own. We sent it to organizations supporting people impacted by the tsunami.

Our actions were small, but they mattered. This showed me a few things:

1. When you see something unfair, you don't have to just watch and do nothing. You don't have to be passive in the face of harm or injustice. You can decide to do something—no matter how big or small. You don't have to let the heartbreak stay inside. You can take action to transform your emotions into something useful. Into something that moves the thing that moved you.

2. Whatever you do matters. Doing something is always worth it.

3. Taking action together has a much bigger impact than doing it alone. Getting more people involved means you'll have the capacity to get more done and more ideas in the mix, which means your plans might expand beyond what you first thought; rather than being able to bake a dozen cupcakes on your own, for example, four people together could make forty-eight cupcakes. Also, the relationships you build with those you do this work with will bring you joy and keep you fighting for longer.

4. Just because something happens far away, it doesn't mean you should ignore it. We live in a global community, and we should respond when asked for help or when we see others in need.

You can't fix or save everything. But whatever you can fix or save will always be worth it. And when it comes to climate action, this is even more true.

Please don't let yourself be discouraged. Don't let yourself become hard. We need your soft heart. We need your courage. I know that you have both already—simply because you're reading this book. Thank you for that. Nurture them. Hold on to them. We can transform so much, together.

4

THE PAST IS STILL PRESENT

So often, if we look only at how things are now and don't look back at the history that made them this way, we end up not understanding reality. If we don't know the past, we can't understand the present.

After we left Jamaica, my parents wanted me to stay connected with my heritage: where I'd come from and the ancestors who had made me. My dad—a white British man, who'd met my Black Jamaican mom at their workplace in Jamaica—was especially keen that I wouldn't lose my Caribbean roots. **He introduced me to the stories of my first hero: Nanny of the Maroons.**

Hundreds of years before I was born, Nanny was a freedom fighter in Jamaica. She ran an army of previously enslaved people—like herself—who would go into plantations and liberate captives. They called themselves the Maroons, and today many of their descendants still live on the territory they won from the British. Through her stories, I learned more about the realities of colonialism.

The word *colonialism* might be new to you, but instead of just telling you the definition and moving on, let's look at it this way:

NANNY of THE MAROONS

Think about your home. You and your family have lived in this home for as long as anyone can remember. Now imagine that one day, someone who has never been there before—and already has a different home elsewhere—arrives at your home for the first time and says, "I've discovered this home! It's mine now! **If you want to live here, you have to do chores all day and night. Otherwise, I will kick you out!**"

This stranger takes all your things and hurts anyone in your family who tries to stop them. They take your bed, your games, your food, and everything else you have. They are a bully.

Even if you do all the chores they force you to do, this

person has also brought diseases with them that you've never seen or heard of before. Your body has no protection from these unfamiliar diseases. It's the same for everyone in your family. So most people in your family get really sick; some even die.

Then more of these strangers start arriving in your house. More of your space is taken, and you're allowed less and less food. One day, you realize you're the only one left of the people who used to live there with you. And the strangers are telling you that you don't belong here. That this is their home, their space, that you were never here before. **That it's always been their home.** It looks nothing like it did before.

Sounds awful, right?

Well, that is *colonialism,* and the people who invaded your home are called *colonizers.* And for so many people throughout history, not only is the story I told a true story, but a far worse one than what's described here.

But at school, we were taught that the British Empire was something to be proud of. That hundreds of years before any of us were born, the British navy and "explorers" set sail from this tiny European island across the ocean to "discover" new lands. We were taught that they "discovered" the land that we now call the United States of America and began to "populate" it with new, European settlers. We were taught that this navy was so strong and mighty that it conquered many lands, making the British Empire the strongest empire in the world. **Other European countries had their own empires,** but we were told to be proud that the British was the best and the biggest.

We were not taught about the Indigenous populations who

already existed in the Americas. We were not taught that colonizers killed entire civilizations either through violence or disease. **Christopher Columbus—and other European colonizers—did not "discover" anything; there were already people there.** And European settlers did not "populate" these lands; they killed or kicked out the populations who had lived there for generations in order to steal the land.

Have you ever wondered why most people in the United States are not native? Why are so many people there now of European descent? Where did all of the Indigenous populations go? If you are Indigenous yourself, perhaps you already know all about what happened. But if you are not, it might be something you haven't thought about.

I remember so clearly the moment I realized the extent to which Indigenous populations in the Americas and the Caribbean had been destroyed. I was ten, and I was working on a project for my geography class. The assignment was to create and deliver a presentation on the geography and history of any country we wanted to. Of course, I chose Jamaica.

I began by speaking to my mom about what she knew about Jamaica. She told me about the Arawak people. **Before Jamaica was colonized by the Spanish and then the British, the Arawak were the Indigenous people who lived on the island.** They called it Xaymaca, meaning "land of wood and water." Jamaica/Xaymaca was their home.

When Christopher Columbus arrived in 1494, the Arawak people had already been living in Jamaica/Xaymaca for over 2,000 years. Columbus and the Spanish began colonizing

Xaymaca, enslaving the native people or killing them with violence and disease. In just a short time, almost all of the Arawak people had been killed by colonialism.

Today, Jamaica is populated by the descendants of Africans, who were kidnapped by European colonists and forced into slavery. While some Jamaicans have Indigenous Arawak ancestry—especially in Maroon communities, because many surviving Arawaks joined the Maroons' fight—the Arawak communities themselves were essentially wiped out.

Colonialism is not just an issue of the past. Its impact bleeds into the present: loss of cultures, people, homes, and livelihoods; borders between countries drawn as lines on a map (look at the African continent!); power dynamics; and financial systems. Its structure is also used as a blueprint for a model called *extractivism.*

Extractivism is the process that fossil fuel companies use to take and extract from the land, and from the communities on the land. Much of the fossil fuel industry's extraction began through colonialism. Shell (one of those big fossil fuel companies we discussed earlier) first got exclusive access to take the oil out of the Niger Delta when the British government literally *bought* the entire country of Nigeria about 125 years ago.

Colonialism never really went away; it just doesn't look the same as it used to. In some cases, like with Israel's occupation of Palestine, it is more obvious. But with others, it's been disguised. Like chameleons and octopuses change their appearance to blend into the background, which allows them to continue to survive, colonialism has morphed and camouflaged itself too.

Fossil fuel extraction has destroyed
large parts of the Niger Delta in Nigeria.

It might not be as easy to see now as it was in the past, but the influence it has on countries and on people is still there.

For example, Shell still operates in the Niger Delta today—polluting the water, air, and land. While Britain may not govern Nigeria any-

Colonialism never really went away; it just doesn't look the same as it used to.

more, the lives of the people who live there are still being made worse so that those who live in richer places—like Europe or the United States—can live more comfortably.

Today, the life expectancy—the average age that people

live to—in the Niger Delta is only forty-one. That's ten years younger than the national average of Nigeria. It might be younger than your parents' age. Meanwhile, in the United Kingdom—where Shell's headquarters are—the life expectancy is eighty. That means that people in the UK live on average almost twice as long as people in the Niger Delta.

In other words, those who live near the concentration of money get longer and safer lives at the top of the hierarchy, while those who live near the extraction of resources that generate that money have half their lives stolen from them.

If we look at our world today, the countries that were historically the colonizers are countries we now call "rich," whereas the countries that were colonized are "poor." **Another way to refer to these different groups of nations is "the Global North" and "the Global South."**

The Global North generally refers to countries in Europe and North America, along with Japan, Australia, New Zealand (also known as Aotearoa, the Indigenous Maori name), and a few others—countries that have hoarded and produced wealth through taking and extracting from countries in the Global South.

The Global South is generally used to refer to regions of Oceania, South America, Africa, and most of Asia—in particular, those that were previously colonized.

While Global North countries might not own or govern these Global South nations anymore, they still have enormous control over them. The most valuable things Global South countries have—their natural resources—are taken from them by companies based in the Global North. Global South oil is used to heat homes in the Global North. Their cobalt is used for the batteries of electric cars in the Global North. Their diamonds are used for jewelry in the Global North. The list goes on and on. Global South countries are left poor, with almost nothing. Because of this theft, they cannot afford to build what they need to protect themselves from the climate disasters already happening where they live.

For example, Pakistan is both one of the countries most affected by and vulnerable to climate breakdown. It is also poor, in part from owing so much money to Global North countries. In August 2022, a horrendous flood submerged a third of the country, leaving one in six people in Pakistan homeless. In the same year, the debt that the government had to pay back rose by a whopping $2.7 billion.

Rather than having money to pay for healthcare and housing for those affected by the 2022 flood or to fund the necessary protections to save people from future floods, **the money goes to some of the same countries that caused this climate crisis.**

Through the lasting effects of colonialism from the past and the power dynamics that continue into today, we are connected to each other, around the world.

5

WE ARE ALL CONNECTED

That was intense, wasn't it? Can we check in again? How are you feeling? If some of this is new information to you, you might want to take some time to process it.

All feelings are welcome here. What's important is what we do with them. I want to remind you that you aren't alone in whatever feelings you're having! Throughout history—and at this very moment—people have learned new things about the past that have changed their perspective on the present. It's one of the most important things we can do, and **it's an experience that connects us all.**

When the mountain feels too tall to climb or the crushing weight feels too heavy to carry, I know I can feel lonely and small. What's helped me, over and over, is knowing that I'm not the first to feel this way. In these times, I like to take a moment to imagine how the people I look up to in history—the people who changed the world so that I can have a safer and freer life—responded to these feelings. How did Nanny of the Maroons or Harriet Tubman react when they were faced with new knowledge about our history and systems that was big, scary, and overwhelming? Did they turn away from it? Try to forget it and continue with the world as it was then? Maybe they did on some occasions.

But there were many times that they decided to face their reality head on. **They chose to channel big feelings into big actions.** That choice liberated countless immeasurably loved humans from violence that's beyond what most of us can understand. That choice inspired countless more to continue to rise up and change things.

We get to make that choice too. That opportunity is one of many things that connects us—past and present, near and far.

Let me tell you about what being overwhelmed in the face of the climate crisis taught me. When I first started to become aware of the enormity of this issue, it would keep me up at night. That's called *eco-anxiety*, and I imagine you have felt it. I was sixteen at the time and making big decisions about my life: from what subjects to study to where to eventually go to college. It felt hard to make these choices not knowing what world I would be inheriting—and if it would even be inhabitable.

I wanted to do something with my anxiety—I was being moved, and I wanted to move the thing that was moving me. So I looked everywhere for what I could do to help.

I came across some social media posts that led me to documentaries about veganism. I learned about the violence that animals are subjected to so that people can eat them. I also learned about the large number of resources needed to produce animal-based foods. All that, and that humans don't even need to eat them to survive. It broke my heart. So I stopped eating and buying animal products.

I wanted to do something with my anxiety—I was being moved, and I wanted to move the thing that was moving me.

I was still awake in the middle of the night, though, so I kept researching and I came across a documentary on the fast-fashion industry, called *The True Cost*. It detailed human rights abuses and the damage to our climate and environment required to make huge volumes of inexpensive clothes quickly. So I stopped buying those kinds of clothes and instead only bought stuff secondhand or from small, "ethical" brands (in quotes because it can be hard to determine what is and isn't ethical, and these words are used to distract sometimes).

But I still couldn't sleep properly—I was still overwhelmed by this enormous crisis—so I did some more research and I ended up in the zero-waste world, a movement that aims for each person to create as close to "zero waste" as possible, particularly plastic waste. I spent a year doing my best to buy everything plastic-free (requiring me to go to five different stores for groceries sometimes), make my own oat milk, and be sure I always had my reusable utensils on me.

I remember sitting down one day and having a wave of eco-anxiety rush over me while I was in the midst of squeezing oat milk—from pulp I'd just blended—in a muslin cloth. I thought, "Everyone in my community can't do this. This isn't accessible to everyone. So can this really be the solution?" I also thought, **"Is this really enough in the face of how big this crisis is?"**

I knew deep down that it wasn't. But I kept trying and trying and trying to reduce my personal impact on the environment. Cutting down here, swapping out there. I was focusing a lot on my personal carbon footprint.

This might be something you've heard of before. **A *carbon footprint* refers to the impact on the climate that each person individually makes through their lifestyle.** In the same way that when you walk through mud and your shoe leaves an imprint in the ground, this footprint refers to the imprint each of us leave on the climate.

It's a very popular idea—the logic is that by understanding our own carbon footprint, each of us can understand what we should change in our lives and reduce the negative climate impacts we have. Sounds helpful, right?

It might come as a shock to you that it was BP—which ranked sixth out of the twenty companies most responsible for the climate crisis—that popularized the term *carbon footprint.* If one of the biggest fossil fuel companies in the whole world is pushing for each of us to focus on our individual emissions, shouldn't we ask ourselves who this idea helps?

While we spend hours squeezing out homemade oat milk, these polluting giants pump millions of barrels of oil from the ground. While we obsess over our individual impacts and sit in guilt, the companies and governments that lock us into carbon-heavy lifestyles are getting away with it.

Sure, some guilt can be helpful—especially for those of us in highly polluting countries. But I don't think it's the best motivator. Plus **it can be isolating** and keep us in our own little bubble, it can distract us from the real culprits (oil companies), and it can make us forget how all of our choices connect us to other people.

The most important lesson I learned from my choices was definitely not about my carbon footprint. It was understanding how inseparable my life was—and is—from the lives of other humans all over the world. I realized that through the clothes I chose to buy and wear, I was connected to the farmers in India who grew the cotton for the material that made up my T-shirts, and the garment workers in Bangladesh who sewed the materials together at the seams.

The food I chose to eat connected me to those who sowed the seeds for soybeans in Brazil, which was then fed to cows, which were then killed for their meat. The food I chose to eat also connected me to the Indigenous people who had been evicted from their lands, which they had lived on for generations, in order for food to be grown on it in their place.

Through the jeans I wore, I was connected to communities who have been sickened due to cancer-causing dyes washing into their water sources. The energy that warmed my home connected me to the workers on dangerous oil rigs, and communities forced to live next to fossil fuel facilities and therefore experience higher rates of cancer and other diseases.

The more I saw these connections, the more I thought my lifestyle changes weren't enough. The more I noticed patterns, the more I saw that they came together as a fabric. And I noticed that, in this fabric, there was a common thread.

That common thread is this: The damage and destruction caused by various industries is inflicted on the countries that were also exploited for colonialism—nations often characterized as poor, even though they are, in fact, rich in natural resources.

These threads also showed me that the *people* being exploited are the same people who still feel the effects of colonialism. That none of the harms being inflicted on the planet or on people are separate from each other. And that the climate crisis is inherently woven into how oppression is hurting the majority of people today.

What this means is that we cannot truly fix the problems of Earth without, at the same time, fixing the problems of our fellow humans who live on it.

6

ROOTS, BRANCHES, LEAVES, AND FRUIT: HOW TO UNDERSTAND INJUSTICE

Let's stay with this idea of everything and everyone being connected. It's really important, but at the same time it can be hard to understand. To understand it better, let's try imagining a tree. . . .

Now, normally when you think of a tree, you might imagine something beautiful or majestic. Trees are often symbols of life or wisdom. But the tree we're going to imagine is . . . different.

Imagine that the wood—of the tree's roots, its bark, its trunk, and its branches—are the oppressive systems of power we briefly talked about. These include racism, extractivism, white supremacy, and sexism.

We are getting to know that all of these systems are interconnected. As the tree goes from its roots to its trunk and its branches, some systems flow to create other systems.

The crises these systems then create are the leaves and fruit of this tree. The impacts of the climate crisis—sea-level rise, droughts, storms, flooding, and more—are some of the leaves and fruit that have grown from these systems.

Other leaves and fruit grow from the same branches, created from the same deeper systems. These are things like police brutality, poverty, hunger, famine, war, and homelessness.

Now let's keep our imagination going with this tree metaphor. So this big tree of injustice in our world isn't alone.

Other systems exist outside of the oppresizve ones, which means that other trees exist, and they also bear leaves and fruit. Some trees' roots, bark, trunk, and branches are composed of good kinds of systems: community, systems supporting each other's needs and in harmony with nature, resource sharing, Indigenous wisdom, and so on.

These systems also overlap and grow from each other. And they produce leaves and fruit. These leaves and fruit are things like thriving ecosystems, connection to each other, safe housing, and accessible and good healthcare.

The problem is, these "good" trees are having their nutrients taken from them by the large tree of injustice and oppression. The tree of injustice and oppression is suffocating the other trees. It's making it a lot harder for the other trees to thrive and grow.

We'll get to how the tree of injustice got so big and invasive later on, but for now, I want us to sit with how we tackle the current scenario: One tree is far too big, its roots are crushing the roots of the trees around it; its leaves are blocking out the sun that would allow the other trees to grow; its fruit is poisoning the ground they fall on. What should we do?

We have options.

We could remove some of the leaves and fruit we don't like—we could try to pluck off the ones that impact the climate crisis. It's the easiest option—it requires less effort right now. That might mean fewer poisoned fruit falling on the surrounding soil, a little more sun shining through to the other trees. We might even manage to get some of the other non-climate leaves and fruit off in the process too.

But the tree will still grow and be there. Its deeper systems will go on producing the same bitter fruit. We haven't really removed the issue; we've just delayed it.

We could chop off some branches, tackle a few of the systems that have branched off from the main ones—the roots—over time. In terms of effort, this is a step beyond just plucking some leaves or fruit. This will remove a lot of the leaves and fruit (symptoms, harms, and impacts) and allow more light in for the other trees to grow, take up more space, and become bigger. This will slow down the growth of the big tree of injustice too.

But the tree of injustice is still there. All of the systems are still there. A lot of the harm is still there. New branches will eventually grow. The tree of injustice is still taking up space and hoarding nutrients in the forest.

So what's our final option? We tackle the roots. We rip them up. We topple the tree, and we allow what's left of it to decompose and compost.

We can work to clean up the bits that would still harm the soil, but we let what nutrients we can use from the tree be repurposed to compost these other systems: the other trees in the forest, the healthy fruit. Space is now there for the other trees to grow. There is space for a new, transformed world to grow.

> **So what's our final option? We tackle the roots. We rip them up.**

Yes, it's still likely that the odd seed from the fallen tree might grow a new sapling every now and then. But they will be smaller than the other trees. They will have less power. It will be so much harder for them to eclipse and consume, like the big tree did before.

Tackling the roots, toppling and composting the tree of

injustice and oppression: that is climate justice work. It's not simple or easy, but it is worth doing. It is also possible.

Work like this, work that goes to the roots of an issue, is sometimes referred to as "radical." The word *radical* originates from the Latin *radicalis,* meaning "of or having roots," and *radix,* meaning "root." In the late fourteenth century, *radical* meant "originating in the root or ground." This is the sort of radical our work for climate justice needs to be. It needs to go to the root of injustice, oppression, and the creation of this crisis, and tackle it there. Topple the tree and rip out its roots; don't just pick off the odd leaf or fruit. We know we can do better than that. And we deserve better than that.

While *radical* may have meant something simple a long time ago, it has gained new meanings in modern times. You might have heard the word *radical* used to mean "extreme," "impossible," "too much," "ridiculous," or "outrageous." I've often been described as radical myself.

Sometimes that is a compliment to people like me in movements for social change: In these spaces, *radical* can often mean "well-read," "willing to push the boundaries," or "brave or wise."

Sometimes it's an attempt to invalidate my work—to make me seem unreasonable. I've been labeled an "extremist" by journalists in the right-wing media for working within my union to create a statement condemning the killing of innocent Palestinian civilians; I've been called "the radical" or "idealistic" by politicians for explaining that we need to transition away from fossil fuels, in line with climate science; and I've been dismissed as "naive" for saying that we all deserve to have access to clean water, safe food, a safe home, and joy in our lives.

Sometimes it's just a reaction from people whose imaginations have been limited by the world as it is. But we cannot let other people's limited imaginations limit our possibilities.

7

IMAGINATION IS POWER!

You might be wondering, "Hey, Mikaela, aren't you veering off course a bit here by talking about imagination? Can we stay on topic, please? Where's the explanation of why the tree of injustice is able to be bigger than all the other trees in the forest?"

Fair point. But we're getting there. Imagination is key here.

Imagine that we haven't toppled the tree of injustice yet, so it's still there. As are the other, smaller trees, with their other branches and their other fruit.

I mentioned nutrients and sunshine before. You might remember from science class that trees need sunshine and water to make food for themselves through a process called *photosynthesis*. They need minerals from the soil for other processes too.

In our tree metaphor, the sunshine is imagination and belief. That is a key nutrient that fuels the trees and allows them to grow. Without it, they die.

Now, most of the sunshine is concentrated on the tree of injustice, simply because it is bigger. Most people believe in its ideas and follow its systems. They believe the systems that power our world right now are fine.

I'm not saying here that the majority of this sunlight is coming from active belief anymore. Some is, but a lot of the sunlight comes from *passive* belief. From people who accept certain things to be "just how the world is." Who don't unlearn or question these systems, because they are submerged in them.

I'm also not saying that the majority even want these systems to exist—let alone the harm they create. This feeling is not based on desire but on the idea that there is no alternative available.

That is compounded by the fact that the big branches of the tree of injustice cover many of the other trees—obscuring them from view and stealing their sunlight, and thereby cutting off imagination and the ability to grow and survive. So there is also a belief that all other systems are unable to be sustained and doomed to failure.

Well, of course they will be if they are not fed or nourished by imagination!

Okay, what do we do with this part of the metaphor? How do we use it to make real change?

Imagination is so important. What we pay attention to grows. What we believe in grows. When we lose belief, when we stop imagining a system as permanent, it begins to die.

It's similar to how in the movie *Elf,* Santa's sled can't fly without Christmas cheer and belief in him.

Right now, the belief most people hold—whether they say it actively or not—is that a world where everyone gets to live in dignity and safety is not possible. That's the sled that gets to fly in our world.

Imagination is so important. What we pay attention to grows. What we believe in grows.

Most people, myself included, were led to believe that there is no alternative to our current economic system—a system we call *capitalism,* and which we will talk more about later. This belief that there is no alternative leads us to act in ways that *prevent the possibility of alternatives.* Believing this idea has made the idea real.

Growing up, I didn't even have words for the systems we live in, never mind the alternatives! Instead, I saw the systems that had already been imagined, constructed, and created as "normal." I accepted our current systems as "just the way things are" rather than seeing them as the realized imaginations of certain people.

Remember when we talked about the different kinds of power—power you can see and power you can't? Well, imagination is something that turns unseen power into real things you can actually see and touch. For both good and bad.

What turns systems or ideas into physical structures? Belief.

Ideas. Imagination. Then acting according to those beliefs and ideas.

Every system, structure, building, and institution in our world first existed only in someone's mind. Their imagination was so powerful that it built this. (Imagine me gesturing at this whole world, the good and the bad, the prisons and the hospitals, the climate crisis and the carnivals.)

Imagination is not just make-believe; it is the beginning of all things. Capitalism is the result of someone's imagination. White supremacy—in fact, the entire concept of race—is the result of someone's imagination. Imagination has been used by those who hoard power to create systems for thousands of years. It is a powerful tool. It's time that those of us who want a better, transformed world recognize that too.

If the imaginations of those in the past were strong enough to create capitalism, our imaginations—our ideas for the future—can be strong enough to make something we want. But it has to begin with us exercising our imaginations.

We started doing that with the tree metaphor. Let's go back to it now.

This time, take a moment and imagine what the best version of your neighborhood would look like in a future where we have won the fight for climate justice. If you can, I'd also like you to get a piece of paper and draw it out, so that you can really visualize it.

This is an activity I did while at the Climate Justice Camp in Lebanon—this one was with over 450 activists from 100 different countries across the world—and I found it to be so helpful. My drawing is stuck up in front of my desk, and I still add to it often!

For your drawing, there are practical things that might come to mind: How would housing work? What sort of transportation would people use? How would people power their homes? You don't have to know all the answers now; this is a living image, which you can change at any time.

There are other questions I want you to sit with too: How would it feel? What would it smell like? What colors would you see when walking around? What sounds would be there? Write down some words that describe these smells, colors, and sounds.

Once you feel like you've created a full picture—whether just in your mind or on paper too—imagine you're in that future now. You're surrounded by its smell. You're swimming in how it feels. Your eyes see those colors. You are there, and it is here.

Now hold on to that feeling. Anchor your soul in that place, in that future. Promise yourself you will believe in it. Promise yourself we'll get there. Once your soul is anchored there, every action you take will be moving us all closer to that future. To the future we all deserve.

As I said before: This is a living image. And it has real power. You can keep amending it and adding to it as you learn more and understand more. One of my favorite anecdotes is one that political activist Angela Davis shared in an interview with the

New York Times. She said: "We didn't include gender issues in [earlier] struggles. There would have been no way to imagine that trans movements would effectively demonstrate to people that it is possible to effectively challenge what counts as normal in so many different areas of our lives."

And the bit that really stands out to me: "A part of me is glad that we didn't win the revolution we were fighting for back then, because there would still be male supremacy. . . . There would be all of these things that we had not yet come to consciousness about."

What she meant was: The world that she was fighting for back then wasn't as good as the world could ultimately be. As Angela spent more time on Earth and met more people, she came to understand that the revolutionary vision of the future that she and other activists had been trying to build was still limited: They didn't yet understand the expansiveness of gender, the experiences of members of the trans community, and what liberation for them would look like too. The liberation Angela had been fighting for then wasn't complete liberation for *everyone.*

I've looked up to Angela Davis for a long time. If you don't know her yet, Angela is a Black feminist and a professor who—in her twenties, when organizing with a political group called the Black Panthers—was wrongfully imprisoned. At the time, the many forms of racism faced by Black people in the US were even worse than now.

In the face of the oppression of Black people, Angela Davis

was part of the Black Power movement. And because those who held power were responsible for the oppression, they were afraid of the influence that Angela and many other Black Power activists had. Many of these activists were jailed or assassinated in an attempt to silence their voices.

Instead, it only worked to amplify them. The campaign to free Angela Davis was huge. She was the most famous political prisoner in the US at the time, and upon her liberation, her ideas spread all over the world.

Her words have had a profound impact on my life. Basically, she's one of my heroes (even if I don't think heroism is that helpful—we'll get to that later). So to hear someone I respect so much—who also knows so much about social justice and transforming our world—admit that their early vision of the future had been limited made it clear that mine must definitely be too.

So will yours. And that's exciting!

Maybe you're thinking, "Wait, why is it *exciting* that my vision is limited?"

It's because the best possible future is *beyond* our current ability to imagine.

So often we are told

ANGELA DAVIS

to tone down our expectations, to limit them. But I think we need to do the opposite. Push the future of your imagination farther, and know that that vision, too, is limited. It's *still* not as good as it gets!

Imagine, imagine, imagine. And act, act, act.

POETRY BREAK

We're taking on some heavy ideas in this book! So it's important that we have a space to breathe now and then. In between each major section of the book, I'll share a poem I've written. Poetry often helps me make sense of the world.

You might remember that I mentioned before that I pretty much only wear pink clothes. I get asked about why I do this a lot. To be honest, I'm still not sure! As usual, when I'm wondering about something, I wrote a poem to help me figure it out. I hope that sharing it here will help you get to know me a little better! And don't worry if you don't understand every word—the more important thing about a poem is how it makes you feel.

PINK

I wear a lot of pink
A lot, a lot
Scroll down my feed and see
Even my stethoscope is pink

I have often wondered where this came from
A large part is that choosing and sticking to one color makes secondhand shopping a lot easier
I just head directly for the pink section and skip everything else

But the questions still linger in my mind
Do I wear this soft femme color in order to subvert the expectations
of what a "strong" Black woman should be?
Or is it a protection mechanism against misogynoir?
Maybe if I wear pink fluffy clothes
Big earrings
Use quirky phrases
then I won't be seen as "angry"?
Spoiler:
It hasn't worked

I think that in a world that wants me to be hard
I hold on to all the soft parts of myself even tighter
I hold on to whatever gives me joy
I'll allow that inner child to roar
to be creative in all the ways she wasn't able to be before
because of
a cloudy mind
anti-Blackness
and school bullies

In the midst of all the serious work I do
I also want there to be lightness
Some of that comes from the clothes I wear
I wear them for me now
And for her back then

PART 2

8

CONSUMED BY OUR STUFF

When you wake up in the morning, you might roll out of bed bleary-eyed, sleep still clinging to the edges of your mind. A lot of times, you might not even want to get out of bed and you try to squeeze out a few more minutes there. Then you might sit down and eat. Maybe some breakfast cereal from lands that used to be covered with sprawling rainforests, which were then deforested to grow grains to be made into flakes, or to grow the sugarcane that makes the flakes sweet. Sometimes you might even be lucky enough to have chocolate chip pancakes, made with cacao that was grown and harvested by farmers paid less and less for their work while the big chocolate corporations make more and more money from selling the products they make with the cocoa beans.

You might change into clothes made in factories where workers are banned from coming together in unions to advocate for their rights, and who, like the fruit pickers and cacao farmers, are not paid enough to be able to afford the food, housing, water, and healthcare that they need to live.

After breakfast, it's time for school. **Perhaps you are driven to school in a car that burns oil,** emitting planet-warming exhaust, or in an electric car whose battery is made with lithium that has been mined in Bolivia, poisoning the only water sources for communities there. Or maybe you take a school bus, where you'll be sharing the planet-warming exhaust with your classmates, lessening the impact of each journey.

Along the way, you might have a look at your phone, which may have microchips in it made from precious minerals in the Democratic Republic of the Congo, where kids are forced to fight in wars.

When the final bell rings at the end of the school day, you're ecstatic. School's out! But how often do you remember the kids halfway across the world who walk hours every day just to get to school?

Okay, time to head home. Maybe you spend some time on social media, as most of us do, which means somewhere far away a data server has to use more power. If it's cold outside, the heat, which may use gas from Indigenous lands, is on to keep the house toasty and comfortable. If it's hot outside, there may be fans, or even air-conditioning, which uses a lot of energy, to keep things from overheating.

I'm in no way trying to make you feel personally judged

or bad here: Remember, guilt will only get us so far! Often, it's more of a barrier than a motivator. **When I realized how my actions connected me to the lives of others and to impacts on others, it made me panic!** That panic came from a place of feeling like I didn't have that much choice over a lot of these things—it all felt so big, and I felt so small. As I explained earlier, the parts I felt I did have a choice over, I tried to control. But the more I did this, the more I realized that even these parts aren't real choices at all.

The real choices that cause most of the harm here—the choice to continue an energy system based on fossil fuels, the choice to make lots of public transportation inaccessible for some, the choice to not pay workers living wages while paying bosses and shareholders millions—are made by big corporations and governments. Focus your energies on tackling them. Channel your emotions there.

If you live an average life in the United States, by the end of a day you are personally connected to—via your lifestyle—more emissions than the average person in the country of Niger is in a whole year. **Less than one day in the US versus a whole year in Niger!**

This is because in countries like the US—Global North countries—consumption is way higher. We use more stuff. **And more stuff is used to make our stuff.** Rather than eating whole foods that were grown locally, most people eat foods with ingredients that were grown far away, transported to a factory and processed, then transported to a supermarket or restaurant and sold to us.

Less than 20% of the world's population consumes 80% of the world's natural resources.

Not all of the food that's grown even gets consumed. Some experts estimate that around 40 percent of the food produced in the United States is wasted. Imagine opening a box of pizza, eating five slices, and throwing the other three slices straight into the garbage. That's how much food we waste!

And our electronic gadgets are a whole different category of waste. Phones, laptops, and other devices are deliberately made to break, made so that they can't be fixed and we have to buy new ones every few years. Experts estimate that forty million tons of electronic waste are generated worldwide each year. To give you an idea of how much that is, **imagine 800 laptops being thrown away every second!**

Cars are also a big part of life in Global North countries, especially in the United States: Having your own car and using it to get around, rather than using public or shared transportation, is normal. This means that on average, people in the Global North consume a lot more fuel than people in the Global South, where car ownership is not nearly as common and public/shared transportation or active transportation—like walking, cycling, or running—is the norm.

Let's say you live on a farm with nine other people. The ten of you have different plots of land that you own and are responsible for. You each rely on the food you grow on your plot of land to feed yourself. But sometimes you trade with the other farmers to get things that only they can grow on their plots of land.

That would be fair, right?

Okay, now imagine that just two of the farmers decide to take all the food from eight of the plots. They aren't "stealing" it, technically. Maybe they offer a few pennies in return, but there is a clear imbalance. You and the other seven people are forced to try to survive off the food from the two remaining plots, whereas these two greedy people have eight plots' worth of food all to themselves. That seems pretty unfair, right?

Well, that's the reality of how resources are distributed in our world. **Less than 20 percent of the world's population is responsible for the consumption of a whopping 80 percent of the world's natural resources.** It's like the story about the farm but on a huge scale. The resources aren't just food and land: They're also water, trees, fuel, aluminum, gold, and diamonds . . . The list goes on and on.

Can you guess where the 20 percent live? Do you think they're mostly in the Global North or in the Global South?

If you said the Global North, you are correct! According to a report from 2012, the 20 percent of the population who consume 80 percent of the world's resources is made up of the richest people in the world—and those people are mostly in the Global North, like in the United States, Europe, or the United Kingdom. **Being rich is very bad for the planet!**

Does this whole deal seem familiar to you? Similar to something else we've talked about? This is a time when understanding the past can help us understand our present.

Do you remember our discussion of colonialism? Colonialism in the past saw a small number of nations take over vast areas of the world. Today, the out-of-balance way resources are consumed echoes that same basic idea. Yet again, a few nations are taking more than is fair from the majority of people in the world.

A few nations are taking more than is fair from the majority of people in the world.

And it's not only about

who gets to have the most resources. It's also about who produces the most greenhouse gas emissions.

In a similar way to how land was colonized in the past, the atmosphere has also been colonized. You might be thinking, "Hold up! What do you mean? How can we colonize the atmosphere when it's just the air all around us in the world?"

Remember when I spoke about how Britain was a big colonizer in the past? Well, while the British took physical lands and countries, they also took up more than their fair share of the atmosphere. In fact, until 1882 more than half of the world's greenhouse gas emissions came from Britain *alone.*

Global North countries have polluted way more than their share. A whopping 92 percent of emissions that cause the climate crisis have been produced by countries in the Global North. And of that, a humongous 40 percent of climate-crisis-causing emissions have come from the US alone. That is wild! So only 8 percent of emissions causing the climate crisis have come from nations in the Global South—the same ones experiencing the worst impacts. It is incredibly unfair.

Making things fair is vital to climate justice. Repairing the harm—and understanding the history—is essential for how we move forward. Given that the US, the UK, and other Global North countries have produced the lion's share of emissions causing this crisis, those countries need to pay the lion's share to fix it. And given that many of these countries also built their wealth through colonialism, it is essential that they return the wealth they took. **It's common sense, right?**

Look at it this way: If your friend or your sibling ran into your room, took your things, and sprayed water everywhere, damaging your stuff, what would you do? What would you think is fair in that situation?

Would you say, "Oh, hey, it's cool, don't worry, that's in the past now—I'm just gonna hang out in this damp, unsafe room with none of my things, because I need to get over it and move on"?

Uhhh, probably not. You'd ask whoever wrecked your things to make it right, wouldn't you?

In a global sense, the concept of making things right is called *reparations*. It means helping the people who were wronged, usually in the form of paying them money. To be clear: I don't mean *you* personally going to another country and giving someone money! I mean our countries and our governments—and the super-wealthy people and companies still living off wealth gained from colonialism—giving money to communities so they can build back and repair damage. Making their homes safer from the impacts of the climate crisis, for example, or building better schools and neighborhoods. Olúfẹ́mi O. Táíwò, professor and author, describes reparations as "a construction project," a way that we can "remake the world."

While wealth was taken to increase inequality, it can be returned in ways that decrease it. What's more, many countries simply do not have the financial resources to be able to adapt to the climate crisis because of colonialism's impacts, so **reparations are more essential now than they ever were.** Debt must be forgiven, and the countries that caused this crisis must accelerate their switch to renewable energy and pay their fair share to make that possible for other countries too.

HEY, IT'S OKAY, I HAVE LOTS OF STUFF TOO!

We're going to think a bit more about all the stuff in our lives, and—same as before—none of this is about judging you or making you feel bad. I have lots of stuff too. Definitely still more than I need! I'm very far from perfect, and no one's expecting or demanding perfection. We are all messy people in our own different ways. But understanding our stuff—where it came from, who it came from, and what resources were needed to make it—helps us figure out what's needed to enable everyone to live better lives. Taking the time to learn can feel like a lot, **but what it does is create space in our minds to imagine bigger, better, and freer futures for us all!**

Knowing this, look around the room you're in as you read this. Look at all the stuff in the room. Maybe there's furniture, electronics, food, clothing, or toys. Next, think about how far these things had to travel to get to you. Where were the trees for the wood grown? Where was the cotton grown? Where was this stuff assembled or sewn together? Who made it?

Now think about the resources required for all of these things. The water needed for the plants to grow, the fuel needed for the ships and trucks that transported things. Start picturing how much that is.

The answer to my next question will very much depend on

your individual situation: Do you actually need everything in the room around you?

If you're at school, maybe each thing in the room has a clear function, or maybe there isn't even enough of what you need. Or perhaps each thing brings you joy in a particular and unique way. The pens will help you learn to write and record your lessons. The paper will do the same.

At home, you also have stuff that serves an important purpose—like your bed, for sleep. But there might also be some stuff in your home that you thought you needed or wanted, and then quite quickly you decided it wasn't that important after all. **There might even be a lot of these things.**

Maybe you saw something in a commercial. Maybe this commercial made you feel like your life would be so much better if only you had this thing.

Has your life been much better since you've had it? It might have been momentarily, but often that feeling wears off.

For me, something that comes to mind is my password journal. When I was around eight or nine, I remember seeing commercials for a journal that would open only to your voice. The commercial showed a girl opening it with her own special word, then writing all her secrets in it before closing it shut so that her little brother couldn't get in. Seeing the ad over and over made me want one *so* badly. I really believed that my life would be much better if I just had this big pink plastic journal!

Christmas morning came around, and Santa brought me

my dream gift. At that moment, I was overjoyed! I spent the day scribbling and doodling in my new journal, writing down who I had a crush on in my class, who my best friends were, and what I was annoyed about. Opening it with my voice was so satisfying—the first few times. But it wasn't long before my little brother overheard my password and worked out how to imitate my voice to get the journal to open. Soon after that, I stopped using it altogether. The paper part of it wasn't very good: In fact, my normal notebooks were much better. The plastic casing made it difficult to carry around and uncomfortable to use. Needing batteries in order to open it was also a pain. Turned out, this thing I'd thought would transform my life only really gave me fun for a couple of days.

Remember how we looked around and thought about the resources for everything in the room around us? Now do that again, but only for each of the things that you think you no longer need or want. For my password journal, for example, oil was extracted to make the plastic covering, minerals were mined for the batteries and metal parts, and much more. If you can't find something you don't need or want in your room, try to think of something that your friends or family members might have that fits into that category.

Kind of a waste, right? All of those resources used for something that turned out to be trash. **Should we find other ways to bring us joy?**

The hope of creating a just and fair and beautiful world, that picture we drew of what that world would look like . . .

those are some things that bring me joy. Organizing with others to build this world—to create this hope—brings me a lot of joy too.

To be honest, lots of the stuff in my life brings me joy. I'm not some activist robot! I love silly pink outfits, **I love a good book,** and my toy dog Doggie brings me a ridiculous amount of joy every day! But the important point here is that we need to find a way to make the things that bring us joy also bring joy to everyone else connected to those things.

For my silly pink outfits, that means getting them secondhand, so that my love of pink clothes doesn't require another woman across the world to work in unsafe conditions or doesn't lead to even more clothes being dumped in a landfill. Perhaps you could start thinking about how to do this with the things that bring you joy.

CHANGES AND CHOICES

Can you guess one of the biggest influences that drives us into the wasteful patterns we just talked about?

Advertising! The attractive pictures and videos we see on TV, social media, and all over the place. Like what happened with me and the password journal, ads trick us into thinking we *need* something—that we don't just want it; we absolutely have to have it! This pushes us to consume far more than we need to, wasting more of Earth's precious resources and making the climate crisis worse.

Think about what *actually* makes you happy. **When have you been the happiest?** What sort of memories are coming up for you?

For me, it's time spent with my loved ones: long walks with my parents, cuddling my family dogs (Simba and Nala), laughing with my friends, reading a good book, swimming in the sea, scuba diving, surfing, or seeing a beautiful sunset. Most of these things don't require me to buy anything at all.

It's important to reflect on what really makes us happy, since so often when we talk about reducing consumption, it can seem like we're asking everyone—and ourselves, in particular—to have less, to be smaller.

While it is true that we'd be buying and consuming less *stuff*, that would create more space for the things we *do* want and need. More time and money to spend connecting with those you love rather than spending it shopping. **More time on this planet. More life.** Consuming less can be about making a life that is bigger—in connection with each other and the land.

Rather than owning everything ourselves and consuming more than we need to, we can share things. It's not this far-off dream—it's a solution that many of us already understand in

> **Consuming less can be about making a life that is bigger—in connection with each other and the land.**

some ways. Perhaps you got this book from a library. If you did, then you're already taking part in a sharing economy!

By sharing the things that are already made, we reduce the need or demand to make more things. And books aren't the only things we can share: We can share tools, cars, and more. Sharing makes the most sense for items that we won't use very often or that we'll only use one time (e.g., reading a book once).

Another way of sharing things is to get things secondhand. Have you had hand-me-down clothes from older siblings or cousins? If so, you've been dressing yourself in the most sustainable and climate-friendly way possible!

The most sustainable clothing that any of us can wear isn't the new stuff that's labeled "sustainable" by big brands: **It's the old clothes.** More than enough garments already exist to clothe every person on Earth for years to come. Fast-fashion companies that make clothes cheaply and quickly—and cut corners on sustainability and workers' wages to get there—are making more clothes every year than it would even be possible to wear! In the US, an astonishing 85 percent of all textiles people no longer want are either dumped in a landfill or burned. Many garments that aren't thrown away are shipped to countries like Ghana, where they have put local tailors out of business. **Clothing waste is so huge globally that**

it's equivalent to a garbage truck full of clothes ending up in a landfill each second!

By dressing yourself in secondhand clothes or sticking with the clothes you already own, you are choosing to give them a longer life and keep them out of the trash. And by using what already exists, you are reducing the impact clothing has on our environment.

The next thing you can do here is to take care of your stuff and then repair and mend it as needed so that it lasts even longer. By doing this, you're stepping away from excessive consumption and into a world where we can live in harmony with Earth.

Let's do another check-in. How are you feeling reading all this? Are you surprised? Sad? Is guilt an emotion that's coming up for you again? Remember what I said earlier: **Not all of that guilt is bad.** A little guilt can motivate us to do better. We *do* need to reduce our consumption in the Global North if we want to meet climate targets, so changing our behavior and consuming less is important. But *too much* guilt is a trap. *Too much* guilt leaves us in a spiral of blaming only ourselves.

I remember so clearly having a conversation with my grandma in Jamaica about the climate crisis and her responding that "it's Mother Nature taking it out on all of us." This is a common way of thinking, the idea that because "we" are causing the climate crisis, "we" are feeling the impact.

But this idea doesn't sit very well with me. Putting the blame on "humans" or "all of us" is far too vague. It feeds into the same cycles of guilt and shame that can be super-unhelpful.

When 100 companies are responsible for 71 percent of climate-crisis-causing emissions since 1988 and the richest 1 percent of the world's population produce more than double the carbon emissions of the poorest half of the world, "we" did not cause the climate crisis. To say any of these catch-all words to allocate responsibility is to let the small percentage of people who are actually responsible off the hook. **We can't afford to do that!**

If the climate crisis really was Mother Nature taking revenge

on those who've caused it, wouldn't it be the fossil fuel execs, the public relations companies that protect their image, the politicians, and the private-jet-flying celebrities who'd be facing the worst impacts? Instead, those who have played the smallest role in causing this crisis are experiencing the worst impacts.

We are not all equally responsible for the climate crisis. We don't all have the same choices—or the same power—over the emissions we are connected to.

In the UK, for most people the action that could do the most to reduce energy usage—and thereby emissions—would be insulating their homes. Houses in the UK are among the leakiest in all of Europe,

> **We are not all equally responsible for the climate crisis.**

and insulation would help prevent this. Most houses have little or no insulation, and heat flows right out.

Okay, so people should get insulation, right? Problem solved!

But, wait, **most people who live in these homes either aren't able to insulate them themselves**—as they are renting and their landlord won't insulate—or they can't afford to. And if people aren't able to afford it, is it really a choice?

When we talk about responsibility, when we talk about consumption, it's not as simple as it might seem at first. Those who can afford to or are able to make more climate-friendly changes should make those changes. We will *all* have to live our lives differently in order to meet climate targets, and we should all be open to change. But a lot of these changes—like insulating homes—aren't accessible to most people now.

So we need to persuade governments to make them accessible, rather than guilting—or putting the responsibility on—the people who don't have a choice in the matter. Basically: **We have to do what we can,** and we have to organize and advocate for climate-friendly actions to be the default, rather than a "choice," which is in reality available to only some people.

Even though we aren't *the* cause of the climate crisis, *we are the solution.* It is on us to direct a new path.

9

A CAPITAL *B* BAD SYSTEM: CAPITALISM

We just talked a whole lot about our "stuff." What we buy, how much other stuff it takes to make our stuff, and how much of it goes to waste.

But why? Why is there so much of everything? Why does it always seem like everyone wants us to buy more stuff?

We learned a little bit about how advertising is really good at making us want things. But that's not the answer. **Advertising is only a small tool behind something much bigger.**

So what is it? What's this bigger deal? Is it one of those shady "systems of power"? Something we can't see but creates real things we can see? Yup, you guessed it!

The big thing behind how much we buy and consume is one of the most important issues for us to understand if we are going to tackle the climate crisis and build climate justice.

It's called *capitalism.*

Have you ever heard this word before? Maybe on the news, at school, or written on placards at protests. If you already know lots about it, you're way ahead of where I was at your age! It took me until university to fully understand what capitalism is, and I'm still learning more every day.

With big words like this, I always find it helpful to break them down.

Let's start with the first part of the word: *capital.*

Do you know what that means? You might think of upper-case letters or important cities or even forms of punishment. **It's a word that can mean a lot of things.**

In this case, though, it's pretty simple. It means "money"! (Okay, it's perhaps a little deeper than that, but "money" is a good starting point for now.)

Now we are left with the *-ism.* What does that mean?

Think about other words ending in *-ism*—there's *racism, socialism, colonialism, imperialism.* As with all of these words, the *-ism* in *capitalism* is showing you that the word is representing a belief, theory, system, or practice.

So it's a theory or system of money? Or relating to money? This is a really good place to start!

There is so much we could say about capitalism, but we're

going to stick to the basics and how it relates to the climate crisis.

While it took me until I was older to know the definition of *capitalism,* **I saw how it operated around me.**

I saw supermarkets filled with food in my neighborhood while people were starving in the countries where much of this food was grown.

In the media, I saw billionaires and hotshot CEOs live luxurious lives while people who worked for their companies struggled to pay for food for their children.

Perhaps you've noticed these things too. In both of these instances, I noticed how **a small group of people had more power and more money** than most of the people who worked in factories or in warehouses, or packed boxes, or drove delivery trucks—all of the things necessary to make the huge profits that fund fancy lifestyles.

The adults in my life would tell me this was all logical. The logic went that those who are CEOs or bosses are smarter, have worked harder, and have more responsibility than those who are working lower-paid jobs. In that way, it was explained to me, the

unequal distribution of money and power in a company was justified.

How does that sound to you? **Does that "logic" sound fair?**

Well, as I got older, that whole idea and its logic started to crumble. Before I went to medical school, I took a gap year to work and travel. For the first six months, I had a job in a nursing home.

I was hired as a caregiver, which meant spending my days helping the residents eat, wash up, get dressed, and stay active. It sounded good to me, since I wanted more experience before medical school. Perhaps one of your parents is a caregiver. Or maybe you have a caregiver come to your home to support you or a family member. Or maybe you provide some of that support yourself for someone in your life. Well, after my first day on the job, I came home completely exhausted.

I was privileged to be living at home with my family, with very few expenses, so I was able to save my earnings to go toward traveling. But my colleagues—many who worked much longer hours than I did—had bills to pay. They had rent to cover. Some also had children to support. They were the hardest-working people I'd ever met at that point in my life, and they weren't being paid anywhere near enough to match how hard they worked. It made me wonder why we value some jobs so highly and deem others to be so much less worthy.

I saw how pricey the care home was for residents. And it's true that it was an expensive place to run—the cost of equipment, food, energy, and more would be a lot. But **I couldn't help but feel that it was very unfair** that the big bosses who owned the company made salaries many times higher than the caregivers, chefs, and cleaners who were doing the hard manual work that kept everything running.

Given that it was the workers doing the heavy lifting to produce the profits, shouldn't they get an equitable share of them? Why did they have to live paycheck to paycheck while the bosses got to live more stable lives in bigger, more luxurious homes? The imbalance and inequality really bothered me.

As I got older, I understood that this imbalance and inequality is a defining feature of capitalism. The bosses at the top of the hierarchy have power and control over the flow of money and resources that others need to survive, and the workers at the bottom of the hierarchy have no power and control; they have to spend whatever wages they're allowed on the things they need to survive, never mind live comfortably.

Under this system, **we are encouraged to compete.** To compete for money, compete for jobs, compete to live in the fanciest house or drive the flashiest car. But in any competition, a few come out on top while many more end up at the bottom. The people at the bottom don't get big houses or flashy cars, and in many cases they don't have the basic things they need to live healthy, safe, and dignified lives.

The more I understood this, the more I started to think that none of this made sense. I asked myself, **"Well, why can't we have a system where no one has to live without their basic needs met, where no one is at the bottom?"** Under capitalism, resources are not distributed—or shared—according to need. They are accessible only according to how much money each person has.

This creates a system where some people have homes filled with more food than they could ever eat while others can't afford to access any food at all.

Lots of people in the world think capitalism is a great idea. And it's not a coincidence that these tend to be the people at the top, with the big houses and all that. "Capitalism is how we are able to get stuff done," they say. "It's an efficient system!" But what if it's also creating a huge amount of waste? Is that really efficient? What if it creates suffering? Is that really a great idea?

For a capitalist system to survive, it needs its money to grow. Money is the fuel of capitalism. And the money needs to not just grow at a steady, slow speed, like a plant or a snail moving forward. For a capitalist economy to be thought of as "succeeding," it has to double its money every 23 years. If it doesn't do that, it fails. In this pursuit of doubling its money, it has to create more stuff to sell. More stuff to sell so that more money can be made.

And you know what that means, right? More fossil fuels are extracted and burned, more carbon dioxide is emitted, and more natural resources are used to make, transport, and sell us stuff.

Capitalism is like a giant python wrapped around us—and the world—squeezing out everything it possibly can. It is that strong and that powerful. And now that I've explained a little bit about what it is, let's end this chapter with a thought about what it means for our future. Simply put, capitalism is fundamentally incompatible with the continuation of human life on Earth.

That's a strong statement, but there's no way around it: For

capitalism to ultimately succeed, the majority of life on
Earth would have to die.

Simply put, capitalism is fundamentally incompatible with the continuation of human life on Earth.

But here's another strong
statement: We don't have to
accept capitalism. We can
change it! We can build a
world where everyone has
enough of the things we need to survive and we aren't destroying the planet.

10

WE CAN CHANGE IT!

In 2023, I went to Ireland to speak at a book festival about my first book, *It's Not That Radical.* The festival was held in the middle of the Irish countryside at a big fancy castle surrounded by fields, with birds singing all around us. Ireland has a history of colonialism: It was colonized by the British, and many people there were starved while food was taken from Ireland and shipped to Britain in what's now known as the potato famine.

Ireland also has a revolutionary history, which made me excited to speak there. Before my event, I decided to sit in and listen to a panel on food systems and the climate crisis. The two older, white men in this conversation were researchers who work for the United Nations, specializing in food systems. Food systems aren't my area of focus, so I was looking forward to learning more.

At first, they talked about why many people around the world are starving and how things could get a lot worse if the climate crisis isn't adequately tackled. Then both panelists said that the reason so many people are starving is that there isn't enough money to go around, and because "the people are poor." The solution they posed was to grow seaweed and feed people with that. Everyone else in the crowd clapped their approval, but I sat completely stunned!

Were they for real? Would everyone who clapped be all right just eating seaweed? Would you? If eating mostly seaweed as your diet sounds pretty repulsive to you, why would it be okay for others?

Have you ever been told—or thought to yourself—that there isn't enough food to go around? Or that the reason people are left unhoused is because we don't have enough houses?

Did you know that more than enough food is currently being produced to feed every single person—all almost eight billion people—on this planet today? And that in the United States, 15 million homes are empty—more than enough to house every homeless person in the country?

In fact, the amount of food wasted worldwide every year could feed *two billion people*—that's more than twice the number of undernourished people in the world today.

I'm not talking merely about the leftovers you leave on your plate when you're full. It's the massive amount of food that is thrown away by supermarkets and restaurants when they don't sell it in time. Some of this food is perfectly good to eat, but supermarkets aren't allowed to sell it when it's gone past its "sell by" date. In the US, a country where one out of every five kids goes to bed hungry every night, because their parents can't afford to buy enough food, you'd think that it would make sense for stores to share this food, right? In fact, many supermarkets instead throw it in the garbage and even lock the bins closed to prevent people from getting it.

Doesn't it seem completely outrageous that we are throwing away food when, at the same time, people are starving? With all of this information, do you still think that the problem is that there isn't enough food? **Or is the problem how it is distributed?**

A lot of starving people happen to live in areas where food is produced. Like in the potato famine in Ireland, food is shipped away from people who are starving to be sold—or wasted—because it is directed by money, rather than by need.

Under capitalism, resources are not distributed—or shared—according to need; they are accessible according to how much money each person has. This creates a system where some people have homes filled with more food than they could ever eat, while others can't afford to access any food at all. So growing a lot of seaweed won't fix starvation: We need to tackle the system itself, which tells us that those who have food *deserve to have it because they have money,* whereas *those who don't have money don't deserve food.*

This false scarcity—the artificial idea that we don't actually have enough—cloaks the reality that resources are actively withheld from those who need them and the fact that we are made to believe that not everyone has a right to the things we all need as humans to survive. **When you think about it, it's pretty messed up!**

Do you think that there's anyone who doesn't deserve to have the things they need to survive? Is it okay for anyone to not have enough water, healthy food, or a safe home?

This might be another moment when you realize that things you've always accepted as "just how things are" aren't good enough, and it makes you feel angry or sad. Hold on to these feelings: Channel them. Don't push them down. Remember, we can use these feelings to change the things that make us feel that way!

ANOTHER WORLD IS POSSIBLE

When the bosses at big corporations sit down to make decisions, they look at a lot of numbers and a lot of charts with lines going up and down. Based on everything we've talked about, what do you think those lines going up and down represent? Do you think the numbers and lines show how people's lives are affected by their decisions? How much drinking water is contaminated by their decisions? How unhealthy their decisions will make people's lives? Or do you think the numbers and lines show how much money their decisions will make?

I have a feeling you already know the answer! Under capitalism, these decisions—the decisions to use up more resources to make more stuff—are made with one thing in mind. You guessed it: money! **It's all driven by money and profits,** making more for themselves no matter how hard they have to squeeze the rest of us. The negative impacts of this kind of growth are ignored. They are rarely talked about in the meetings. There are no charts with lines showing the human costs of all of this.

Cutting down rainforests to mine for coal is more profitable than leaving them alone. The fact that leaving them alone is better for humans' well-being—because they produce oxygen for us to breathe and remove carbon dioxide from the atmosphere—is not something capitalism prioritizes or even factors in at all.

It might seem like this makes no sense. Why does money mean more than our lives? What's the point in being rich if it means the planet will become unlivable? Why would you want to be rich at the expense of the lives and livelihoods of your fellow humans? Why haven't we changed this?

Well, lots of people around the world have challenged and *are* challenging capitalism. This work to challenge capitalism is called *anticapitalism*—that's how I often describe my climate work!

Like with some of the other systems we have chatted about, capitalism is able to continue to be so powerful because most people don't fully understand it. Most people accept it as reality instead of challenging it as something that was made in the past and can be unmade in the present.

Lots of people around the world have challenged and *are* challenging capitalism.

I'm not saying that people actively think, "I accept capitalism as our only reality!"; it's more that people don't actively think about it at all. They think it's just the way things are. Before these last few chapters, had you given it much thought?

Similar to the way that our hearts beat and we breathe in and out because of automatic signals in our brains and muscles, many of us accept capitalism as reality without stopping to think. And **if we don't think a deep breath is possible, we will keep on taking shallow breaths.**

Imagining beyond the "reality" of capitalism, envisioning a

freer, safer, and more dignified future for all, is like choosing to take a deep breath when you've been used to shallow ones. At first, it has to be an active process. You have to stop and think, rather than run on autopilot. It might feel uncomfortable, but the more often you take these deep breaths, the more relaxed it gets and the more relaxed you feel. With more oxygen flowing through your body, you feel more awake and more alive than you did before. After some time of practicing these active deep breaths, the breaths you take without thinking are deeper than they were before. You have recalibrated your body to have space for more. That's what we need to do with our brains and our minds to build a future outside of capitalism.

I can't and won't give clear-cut, concrete answers or solutions to every single problem. I won't tell you there is only one way out of capitalism, because **there are many ways out.** What I can do is give you examples of ways out that people are forging today. One that brings me a lot of inspiration is an Indigenous-led movement in Mexico called the Zapatistas.

Members of the Zapatista movement have built a community in the Chiapas region, where they govern themselves independently from Mexico's larger federal government. Since they took control of the region in 1994, the Zapatistas have created their own system of education, health, justice, Indigenous government, and security—outside of capitalism. Decisions about how they live are made by the members of the community, based on what they need to be well, not based on the desires of big businesses to make profits or governments to increase the growth of the economy. As one of the Zapatista movement's representatives said in an interview, "The base of our society is people, not the capitalist system." **They have been living outside of capitalism for more than thirty years,** inspiring people all over the world and showing clearly that another way of living is possible.

In Rojava, an independent zone north of Syria, members of the community have built an economy based on feminism, sustainability, and the well-being of all people, rather than money and growth.

When it comes to resisting capitalism, people in the Global South are leading the way. We have a lot to learn from them, about the societies they have already built and the ones they are building today. An anticapitalist economy is not just a dream; **in some places, it is already a reality!**

This might all sound big and overwhelming and intense. Alex O'Keefe, a TV show writer, has a useful way of describing it.

In an interview, Alex said that when we tell people that capitalism is bad and they need to challenge it or leave it, we're asking them to leave a boat that they know and have lived on, and jump into the sea. Of course a lot of people don't want to jump: They don't know if they'll sink or swim. They aren't reassured that the water is any better than the boat. The boat is familiar safety.

So for us, as people who are ready to swim in the water, who have prepared for the jump and have learned to swim, our job is to build lifeboats. **Our job is to build security so that people feel like they can jump and they won't drown.** To lower the risk.

What are these lifeboats in the real world? To understand that, we have to understand what it is in the real world that makes people afraid of jumping away from capitalism: Many people are afraid they won't be able to feed their family, have a safe home to live in, and have stability, healthcare, community, and joy in their lives.

How can we provide these things for each other? We build strong communities. We create networks of people who look out for and support each other, rather than abandoning them. We share resources, from food to tools to knowledge to money, to ensure that everyone is safe and no one is left behind. That way, leaping from the boat into the sea isn't as scary, because those who do leap know that they will be held and safe.

These might seem like small actions in the face of a big system. Don't forget: If we all take small actions toward building stronger communities, they will add up to a greater whole. The small becomes big when each of us, together, plays our part.

Our work has to become big. In the face of the challenges ahead of us, big, radical change is what's needed, rather than small, baby-step change. Because using paper straws instead of plastic straws isn't going to fix everything, right? And one of the amazingly great things about climate justice is that the big solutions we need to survive are also solutions to help us thrive.

Moving beyond capitalism will give us a world where we all live freer and more joyful lives, while also tackling the climate crisis. We can have warmer homes, better healthcare, more free time, shorter workweeks, more accessible and healthier food, better and cheaper public transportation, and so much more. Moving beyond capitalism would also reduce our energy consumption! It's a trend we see with a lot of climate action, and **the benefits that arise alongside the expected outcomes are called *co-benefits*.**

When we center justice in climate solutions, we can choose the ones that have the best co-benefits: Insulating homes reduces energy consumption *and* makes home heating affordable. Measures to reduce air pollution from cars *also* keep more kids from falling ill or even dying from asthma. Scientists have found that eliminating fossil fuels from the UK's energy system would likely prevent 20,000 new cases of asthma and 43,000 premature births! It's the best of both worlds: We are fixing the climate crisis *and* saving and improving lives.

How do we determine which of these co-benefits is the "best" to prioritize? This is where understanding health is so important.

An expert in this area named Hilary Graham frames it this way: "Social inequalities become written on the body as *health* inequalities." **What does that mean?** It means that if you are digging up someone's land and poisoning their drinking water, then you are also destroying their bodies. And it's something you can actually see, for example, in pictures of malnourished people from exploited lands.

Remember how we talked about how everything in our world is connected? This is but another example. Our health is a reflection of the social inequalities we face. So if we tackle the things causing ill health, we can also tackle inequality. If we choose climate solutions that have co-benefits that improve health issues, we will be tackling social inequality at the same time.

Like we talked about before, the issues in our world are like one piece of fabric, each thread woven into the next. **You pull on one string, and the rest unravels.**

The visionary writer and poet Audre Lorde once described it like this: "There is no such thing as a single-issue struggle because we don't live single-issue lives." Meaning we can't fix only part of a problem, because problems do not exist in isolation!

It's not just me saying all this about climate and health. One of the biggest and most respected health journals—the *Lancet*—also understands this. In its report from 2009, the Lancet Commission on Health and Climate Change described climate change as "the greatest threat to global health of the 21st century." But only a few years later, the journal reframed this to "the greatest opportunity for global health." This change was made because of these same co-benefits we've been discussing!

How much more exciting is it to be moving *toward* an opportunity, rather than *away* from a threat?

Changing one word—from *threat* to *opportunity*—might seem small, but the effect on our perspective is huge! How much more exciting is it to be moving *toward* an opportunity, rather than *away* from a threat? How does that one tiny switch change how you think about this crisis?

We have the opportunity to transform everything: to wave goodbye to capitalism and hello to an economic system that works for the planet and everyone on it. We have the opportunity to create a new world. Let's do it together!

11

A DIRTY BUSINESS

Have you ever heard someone say that the climate crisis isn't real? Or maybe you've heard someone express doubt that it's as bad as it is or that it's being caused by human activity.

Maybe you've become frustrated with people who say things like this or gotten into some heated discussions or arguments. I know I have. Sometimes it's been with cousins who like to play devil's advocate. But I haven't met many people who don't believe the climate crisis is real. The people who *do* disagree are mostly strangers I've met on the street when giving out leaflets or at a protest—they've quickly and loudly shared their opinion that what I am doing is pointless and then walked off. It's one thing for a stranger on the street to be rude. That is to be expected sometimes. **Occasionally, though, I am disappointed by people I think should know a lot better.**

In 2021, I was in Glasgow for COP26—the big international UN climate conference where I first met Kato. I was walking around inside the conference center when I spotted a senior politician from the UK's Labour Party. He'd been pretty good on climate policy, so I went up to say hi and to ask if we could have a meeting to discuss how he could support some campaigning we were doing around stopping oil fields in the UK. He agreed, and I was excited at the opportunity.

A group of us met with him and his team and explained the importance of stopping new oil and gas projects, given the most recent science showing that we can't have any new oil and gas fields if we want a future we can live in. But the excitement and hope I had felt before the meeting shattered when the politician responded by saying that stopping all new oil and gas was "unrealistic" and it wasn't something he could support.

My heart fell to the pit of my stomach. I asked him how he could decide that doing what needs to happen to protect my birth island from being destroyed by hurricanes and rising sea levels is unrealistic? **Wasn't it his job to make these things realistic?**

It can feel really emotional for us when we care about an issue so much and the people we look up to don't understand or—worse—they reject the reality of what's happening or what needs to be done. I cried a lot after that meeting, but I've recovered since, because I refuse to let that politician's limited imagination or energy limit mine.

In these instances, it can be easy to want to blame the person in front of you for the problems: It's *their* ignorance, *their* refusal to act, *their* decision to side with the fossil fuel companies. **I have felt all of these things.**

I'm not going to say it's totally fine for people like this to go on with their denial, or that none of that is their fault, or that they can't help it that they understand the world the way they do. But these people aren't the real problem. Too often we are led into making either/or judgments about people, thinking of them as wholly bad or wholly good. I think this is completely misleading.

To understand why I'm even saying any of this, **we first need to understand something called *climate denial.***

Like we did with *capitalism,* let's break down the term.

Climate is in reference to the climate crisis and climate change.

Denial is refusing to accept the reality of something.

Together, *climate denial* simply means a refusal to accept the reality of the climate crisis. But that isn't the whole picture.

To fully understand climate denial, we're going to have to jump into my time machine again, this time heading to the 1970s.

Fossil fuel giant Exxon (now known as ExxonMobil) has decided to open a separate office to explore the future of energy. The company hires some of the best scientists in the field and brings them together to look at the impact of renewables (like solar and wind energy) and fossil fuels on our climate. Through their own research, Exxon's scientists find out that continuing to burn the fossil fuels the company was producing could have a devastating impact on our planet, even making vast parts of it unlivable.

What would you have done in this situation? Imagine that you've found out that what you're doing is going to kill Earth and the billions of people on it. Would you continue as normal? **Would you share this information with others?**

Keep in mind that scientists had this information about fifty years ago! Like, maybe before your parents were even born.

It might seem pretty shocking—and it is to me every time I hear it—but Exxon executives chose to keep it all a secret. They hired the best people they could find to distract attention away

from the devastating truths they had found about their own products. And so, climate denial was born.

Billions of dollars have been spent on manipulating both the public and politicians to question the accuracy of climate science. Billions of dollars—over decades—have been spent to make people doubt the science or feel despair and disempowerment about the crisis. These companies have hundreds of people whose *only* job is to try to make you think that nothing is wrong, that everything is fine.

> **These companies have hundreds of people whose *only* job is to try to make you think that nothing is wrong, that everything is fine.**

This is why I think we owe some compassion to the everyday people we get frustrated with. So much has been invested in making them hold on to the beliefs they do—beliefs handed to them from an industry that profits from our destruction. It is going to take a lot of work from all of us to counter it.

It's important to understand that choosing to bury the climate science wasn't the first time fossil fuel industries chose to devalue life. Their existence and horrible practices have been based on dehumanization from the beginning.

Remember when we talked about hierarchies and the idea that some people's lives matter a lot less than others? Well, the fossil fuel industry needs these hierarchies to survive. It was born from and thrives on hierarchies and dehumanizing those at the bottom of them. In particular, **it thrives on hierarchies around race.**

Something you might have learned in school already is that race is just an idea invented a long time ago. It is a concept used to identify a group of people who share physical attributes, like skin color. Race has no real meaning other than the meaning people invented for it. It was made up to justify the practice of slavery. One of the consequences of classifying people by race is that it created a system of power that said one race is supreme over another. **This particular system of power—and it's a big one—is called *white supremacy.***

White supremacy basically says that those classified as white, or those who are thought of as being the closest to "whiteness," are the most human and that those farthest away from whiteness are less human—and therefore less deserving of resources, dignity, and life in all its fullness.

White supremacy was created to justify profiting from the dehumanization of non-white people. Today, it serves this same function: to justify stripping resources from and exploiting many of those same people. And fossil fuel companies are some of the biggest culprits when it comes to exploitation.

In our world today, the majority of exploitation of people and land happens in countries in the Global South—countries mostly populated by non-white people. The extractivism of the fossil fuel industry is so devastating that many places where their extraction happens have been labeled as *sacrifice zones.*

That means exactly what you think it does, that it's okay to "sacrifice" whatever and whoever is there in order to extract fossil fuel. How gruesome is that?

One of these sacrifice zones is the Niger Delta, one of the most polluted areas in the world, where rivers that once were filled with life are now filled with oil and death, and people's lives have been made shorter and their health destroyed by oil extraction and burning off the unwanted gas that is released in the process, also known as *flaring*.

Another is the Cerrejón mine in Colombia. It's the largest open-pit coal mine in Latin America (it's bigger than Paris!), and it's located on the ancestral land of the Wayuu and Yukpa Indigenous communities. The people who lived on these lands for generations are now unable to survive as they did before the mine. Now they are forced into poverty and poorer health. In this area, more than forty children are dying every year due to malnutrition and the impacts of mega-mining on their water access. The Yukpa have even been termed by some academics as being under threat of total extinction.

These areas—these groups of people—are being sacrificed for the comforts and profits of the Global North. Like with colonialism, Black, brown, and Indigenous people are being exterminated in the name of capitalism. Shell, TotalEnergies, Chevron, BP, and other big fossil fuel companies have been accused of, investigated for, and even taken to court for countless human rights abuses and environmental destruction.

Don't you think **we deserve so much better than this?** That the children of the Niger Delta region and the Yukpa and Wayuu people deserve better than this?

Don't forget: We can *all* have better than this. The world has been transformed before, and it will be transformed again. Almost every single change in history has been looked at as "impossible" or "idealistic" before it actually happened. Once a change does happen, people always act like they knew it was coming, as if it were inevitable. Together, we have the power to make these "impossible" changes inevitable. I really believe we will do that!

So then how can we get fossil fuel companies to change? **What if we ask nicely?** What if I mail them a polite letter that says:

Dear billion-dollar oil company,

Please stop harming people.
Thanks in advance.

Love, Mikaela xoxo

Do you think the CEO would read such a letter and say: "Wow, this Mikaela, she asked *so* politely that we are going to immediately stop all of our dehumanizing and evil practices!"?

Hmm, no, I don't think so either. **Millions of people have been asking nicely** since the 1970s, but the oil companies don't listen.

In that case, what can we do? How do we act? How do we take steps to make the beautiful world we've imagined a reality?

12

PAINTING THE WORLD GREEN

We've tried asking nicely, and it hasn't worked. No one responded to our very polite letter. So what do we do now? We have to get working on other tactics!

I think a good way to think about this is to think about what you do when you're trying to convince your parents or caregivers to let you do something. Asking nicely is probably the first step, right? **It's the best first step and sometimes it can be that easy.**

But if you've asked nicely a few times, do you just give up?

Say you want to get a puppy. First, you might ask nicely a few times. If that doesn't work, maybe next time you come prepared with a bunch of facts and figures about why a puppy is such a good idea for you and your family.

The more you ask, the more creative and well researched you might get with your argument. Perhaps you bring in other family members to show their support. If you can get them on board, your case seems stronger. If you get aunts, uncles, and grandparents on board too, this shows that your support is wide-reaching and increases the pressure. But if all this asking nicely fails, what's something else you might do?

When I visit schools to talk to kids about climate, I often ask them this same question. One school was even nice enough to name a classroom after me! When I asked this question to the students in "the Loach class," many of them answered, **"I try to annoy them into it!"**

This is actually a brilliant, and sometimes very effective, strategy! And we can use it against the fossil fuel industry—and other climate-wrecking industries—too.

If we make it really difficult for the people causing the destruction of our home to keep destroying our home, then it's more likely they'll stop doing it.

When it comes to fossil fuel companies, there's something else we can do: **take away their social license.** *Social license* is another key term in this fight for a better future.

To understand what *social license* is, we need to think back to the climate denial campaigns that the fossil fuel companies started decades ago.

These campaigns included advertisements aimed at under-mining the reality of the climate crisis and ads that simply focused on the importance and permanence of fossil fuels. There were sponsored articles in newspapers—presented as opinion pieces—which questioned renewable energy and, again, drummed in the idea that we *needed* fossil fuels. And there were people hired by the fossil fuel companies whose only job was convincing politicians to do what the companies wanted.

Do you know someone who is learning to drive a car? They are studying all the rules and practicing so they can take a test and get their driver's license. A driver's license gives you permission to drive. **A social license is a form of permission too.** But it's the kind of license you can't see. It's not a little plastic card that goes in the wallet of a fossil fuel company CEO to let them do awful things. It's similar to a system of power, one that says, "Hey, this company isn't that bad. In fact, we kind of need them, right? So let's let them go about their business. It's better that way."

This social license is worth *everything* to these companies. Their existence depends on it. It's what keeps people quiet about them.

And did you know that some governments in rich countries, including the US, *give money directly to fossil fuel companies* to help them out? Those same governments also let them pay less in taxes than they should. So instead of collecting taxes from the fossil fuel companies—money that could be used to fund schools, healthcare, and other things that could improve the well-being and social good of all of us—money gets paid to these already multibillion-dollar companies. Doesn't that seem completely ridiculous? But have you ever even heard anyone complain about it?

There is actually very little pushback. There are many

reasons for this—most people not being aware is one of them—but a key reason is the fact that this social license leads so many of us to believe that in some way, the money given to fossil fuel companies is justifiable because "this industry *needs* to exist."

This belief that the fossil fuel industry is permanent, a force as fixed and solid as a giant mountain—**it's a myth!** And it's so important for us to bust this myth. Once we tackle this—once we remove the industry's social license—people will come together to take them down.

While climate denial is now much less of a strategy for these companies, they still do all they can to maintain their social license. Their new strategy is much more subtle, much more like a sly snake rather than the obvious beast of climate denial. **This strategy is *climate delay*.**

Rather than outright lying, saying that the climate crisis isn't real and denying the science, climate delay whispers in our ear that we don't need to be doing so much, that we can take our time: "We don't have to be reducing emissions today. That can wait thirty years!" "We don't need to have a green and just transition right away. We can do that twenty years from now!" It's what that politician at the climate conference in Glasgow was doing.

This is still a lie, of course, but it's a sneakier one. So we really need to understand that **climate delay is still climate denial**. To say that we can push these important science-based deadlines and dates farther and farther into the future is *a denial of the science* that is telling us when we need to make these changes in order to prevent worst-case scenarios we can't come back from.

I think that climate delay is even more dangerous than climate denial, because it seems so reasonable. It's tempting to think we can push things back a bit farther. It seems gentler. But, in fact, it's equally deadly.

A way that fossil fuel companies attempt to keep their social license today is through something called _greenwashing_. You might have heard of this before—like with other terms we've chatted about, you may have seen it on social media or on placards at a protest, or

> **It's tempting to think we can push things back a bit farther. It seems gentler. But, in fact, it's equally deadly.**

discussed it at school or in a climate group. Greenwashing is basically the fossil fuel industry's catfishing tactic. It's how oil companies represent themselves as much more environmentally friendly than they really are.

Do you ever see an advertisement from a company that sells gasoline or oil that actually shows gasoline or oil? I doubt it! It's more likely they show you a nice, clear sunny day with a car driving down winding roads, lined with flowers, past a bunch of wind turbines.

You'd be forgiven for thinking that fossil fuel companies are amazing renewable-energy companies that take good care of the environment and their workers.

This is greenwashing! What they don't tell you in these ads is that renewable energy makes up less than 10 percent of their business activities, with the remaining 90 percent still being fossil fuels. What they don't show you are the rivers that will never sustain life again after being polluted with oil. They don't show you the communities who no longer have safe drinking water due to a pipeline running through their only source. They don't show you the workers who get laid off when the extraction is done. They don't show you Kato's home underwater as a result of extreme weather events and rising sea levels—all as a result of burning fossil fuels.

If their advertising campaigns showed us the whole truth, do you think people would still want to support them? Would you want to? **Or would you want to start trying to take away their license to do these kinds of things?**

Advertising isn't their only dirty trick. They also love telling us about false "solutions," which mislead us into thinking there's an easy way out of the climate crisis. Ever heard of something called *carbon capture*? Imagine flicking on some big fancy machine that magically sucks all the emissions and planet-warming bad stuff out of the air and stores it safely in a box. Isn't that how they trapped the ghosts in *Ghostbusters*? Maybe that works in a movie, but **there's little chance carbon capture can work in real life at the level that fossil fuel companies want you to believe.**

Then there's something called *carbon offsets*. I won't go into too much detail, but it basically means, for example, that you can buy a plane ticket, and then someone else—far away—will do something like plant a tree to offset, or make up for, the emissions from your plane. Sounds like a nice idea, but it turns out that a lot of the time, the plant-a-tree part of the deal doesn't ever happen. And when it does, it often isn't a good deal for the faraway places where it is planted.

And what about replacing every gasoline-fueled car with an electric one? Well, manufacturing new electric cars and transporting them across the world would still produce enormous amounts of emissions. Also, the extraction of **huge amounts of minerals, like lithium, are needed to produce the batteries.** The extraction of this key mineral has already caused horrendous harm to communities, ecosystems, food production, and water access for people living in Bolivia and Chile.

All of these "solutions" seem miraculous at first glance: They don't require us to really change the world that much, merely swap some "greener" things in and some polluting things out. They seem easy. People often get sucked in by them because of this. In reality, these so-called solutions don't solve much.

Remember our tree metaphor? Things like carbon capture and carbon offsets are like snipping a few leaves or twigs from the tree. Rather

These so-called solutions don't solve much.

than going to the *root* of the climate crisis, they paint everything green instead, so it looks nice without fixing much.

When we understand climate justice, we understand that we

can't leave anyone behind in our climate work. Solutions that slap a Band-Aid on problems, that exploit people, that oppress people or cause harm to them are *not real solutions.* We have the opportunity for so much better than this! Transformation of our world for the better of all of us *is* possible.

So what do you think we need to do now? If fossil fuel companies are painting themselves green to prevent us from seeing the reality of what goes on inside, we have to scrub off the paint! We have to challenge their greenwashing wherever we see it, *and* we have to speak the truth of their actions. We have to damage their social license bit by bit, day by day, until no one believes the fossil fuel industry is permanent or necessary, and the majority see its violence and harm for what it is.

When you see greenwashing happening—perhaps on social

media, at an event, or at your school—**have the bravery to say "This isn't true!"** Speak about what the truth actually is, what the impacts these industries are having actually are. You can share this to your class, to your teachers or parents or family members, or online.

And there are creative ways you can do this! Some people have challenged greenwashing advertisements by creating a new version of the ads that includes the reality of what these companies are doing. Others have gone along to conferences or other events where greenwashing is happening to disrupt or protest there so that attendees are shown the reality.

Next time you see greenwashing, think about how you could challenge it—either in ways similar to the examples I've shared here, or come up with some ideas of your own!

This won't be the first time that social license has been taken away from an industry.

Only a couple hundred years ago, the slave trade industry had social license to exist. It was widely accepted in Europe and North America that the enslavement of human beings was necessary or not that bad. It was an accepted industry. But— through campaigning, boycotts, disruption, sabotage, legal challenges, and many more tactics—the industry that profited from enslaving human beings lost its social license.

Today, as it should be, enslavement is seen as an abhorrent and disgusting practice. But **for it to be viewed as such took time, tactics, and people power.**

The tobacco industry is another one that is gradually losing its social license. Back in the 1970s, smoking cigarettes was super-super-common. The damaging health impacts of smoking weren't well known to the public then, and people smoked in hospitals, in schools, in movie theaters, and more. The tobacco industry used the same tactics—of denial and delay—that the fossil fuel industry has used and is using today, to prevent the majority from paying attention to the dangerous health impacts of smoking cigarettes. In fact, the fossil fuel industry has even hired some of the same people who worked with the tobacco industry!

But the tobacco industry didn't win. After only a few decades of campaigning, cigarette smoking is down almost 50 percent from its heyday in the 1970s and 1980s, and the tobacco industry is no longer seen as permanent or not so bad. **That's a real win for campaigners!**

It's now widely understood that smoking is bad for your health: There are warnings on cigarette packets, restrictions on where you can smoke, and limits on the advertisement of tobacco products. None of that happened spontaneously as a result of the science coming out about these products: The tobacco industry pushed back, and so campaigners had to push back. We can—and must—do this to the fossil fuel industry too!

We can't rely on the mere existence of science to save us. We have to act. We have to fight. You'd better believe that billion-dollar corporations—and the politicians in their pockets—are going to fight. But we have *so* much power to fight back, to fight for life, joy, and our future. While fossil fuel companies invest their billions in greenwashing campaigns and social license lobbying, we will invest ourselves—as people—into achieving a present and a future that everyone on this planet deserves. It has been done over and over in the past. We can do it now as well.

So let's take down their social license. Let's call out their greenwashing. **Let's annoy them** so much that it's so difficult to cause the harm their business models necessitate. Let's take down the fossil fuel industry and build an energy system that puts people before profit.

Like with the sharing economy and anticapitalist movements, an energy system that puts people before profit isn't just a faraway dream: **It already exists in some places.**

In Bethesda, a town in Wales, an organization called

Energy Local has worked with more than 100 households to create a club that partners with the local hydroelectric plant. The partnership has allowed residents—in an area with significant fuel poverty—to access cheaper energy directly from the local hydro plant, bypassing big companies and their higher prices. This project has provided a huge benefit to the people who live there!

In Northern California, an Indigenous-, Black-, and queer-led collective of land protectors is building its own solar energy micro-grid. Members of this group are doing this because their main energy supplier—Pacific Gas and Electric—frequently cut off their energy during wildfires and storms. By having control over its own energy supply, one of the collective's members, Nikola Alexandre, said, "We'll shift from a community that is vulnerable to one that is more independent and sovereign in how our energy is produced and used." Energy will be run and provided with the community's needs at the center, rather than being directed by someone else's profits.

Part of how these industries that cause harm to all of us and our environment win is by making us believe that there are no alternatives. In the same way that many of us have come to believe that capitalism is the only reality, we can end up thinking the same about the fossil fuel industry. We have to challenge this idea at every corner! **Other realities are possible.** Other realities are being lived out across the world. We can build them here too—wherever *here* is for you. As writer

Arundhati Roy puts it, "Another world is not only possible, she's on her way. . . . On a quiet day, if I listen very carefully, I can hear her breathing."

I see the alternatives that are already here, already being built around us, as this new world's breath.

13

UP AND DOWN THE STREAM

You've used your imagination to feel the breath of the new world and to see the interconnected systems of power and oppression in our world as trees in a forest. Now let's use it again to **imagine a stream.**

This stream has water flowing in one direction: from the top of a mountain to the bottom. Imagine a person—let's call them Tom—who lives farther down the stream, and that's where Tom gets his water to drink. Sadly, Tom gets diarrhea and vomits a lot. Tom is super-sick, so he goes to see a doctor, who gives medicine to Tom. This medication pauses the vomiting and diarrhea, and means that Tom doesn't die in the short term. It's an important role, because it saves Tom's life in that moment. It prevents Tom from dying then and there.

But while Tom feels better in the moment, he isn't actually cured. Tom still finds himself throwing up and on the toilet for long and painful times after drinking the water from the stream. The doctor keeps giving him medication every time this happens, and the cycle repeats.

I used to see myself as the doctor down the stream: saving people's lives in the moment.

But if we zoom out and look farther upstream, we see something interesting. There's someone throwing bags of poop in the water! And a corporation has started drilling for oil up there too. Poop—and the germs that come with it—and oil and chemicals are all mixing into the water that eventually flows downstream. How gross is that!

Seeing the zoomed-out picture, what do you think is the best thing we can do to help poor Tom, who keeps getting sick?

Should we focus on giving medicine to the people down the stream? That would save Tom and his neighbors' lives in the short term, but their lives would still probably be shorter than they should be, since they'd still be getting sick over and over. It also would feel kind of wrong to just patch them up and send them back out into the same conditions that made them sick in the first place, right?

In that case, **we should go upstream** instead and stop the person from throwing poop into the stream. This would tackle the root cause of the problem—it would stop the thing making people sick in the first place. There wouldn't be such a need for people to visit the doctor, and their lives wouldn't be made shorter by frequent vomiting episodes. Seems like a better solution.

So how do we do that? We can ask the person responsible to stop putting poop in the stream—sometimes simply asking works! We can explain to them what the poop is doing to the people downstream: the health impacts and more. If they don't listen to that or deny that what they're doing is causing those impacts, we could show them more concrete proof via studies or research.

If they still don't stop, maybe you could make it hard for them to put the poop in the stream. **There are lots of ways you could do this:** You could stand in front of them while they are throwing the poop, you could offer somewhere else for them to put it, you could stop them from accessing the water, or you could make it so annoying for them to put the poop in the stream that they finally give up and go away.

A few years ago, I was the doctor at the bottom of this stream. I was the one giving Tom his medicine to help him not feel so sick. I went to medical school. I worked in hospitals on my placements during the COVID-19 pandemic. I thought the best thing I could do was to be a doctor and save lives. But balancing the demands of medical school with my activism work was too much. It left me burned-out and exhausted. And many of the patients who I saw were sick because they had unsafe housing or not enough access to healthy food, or because they didn't have enough money to allow them to live a healthy and safe life.

Now **I see my role as a full-time activist as being more up-**

stream. I want to stop the things that make people sick in the first place. I want to stand *in front of* the person throwing the poop in the water and say, "No, you can't do that," to prevent as much of it as possible from getting in there in the first place. I want to help make a world where no one gets sick because of a system that makes it that way.

When I explained this analogy to the kids in the Loach class, one kid said, "Well, doesn't that mean they just throw poop on you?"

> I want to stop the things that make people sick in the first place.

It's true! Doing the work I do now does mean that sometimes I get poop thrown on me. Sometimes going to the root cause can be messy. But it's so worth doing.

While I might not directly be working as a doctor anymore, **my work is still health work.** I do the things I do because I want us all to be well. I want to make people better, *and* I want to stop people from getting sick in the first place. But now I see that I can more fully perform my role farther upstream.

In fact, it was viewing systems of oppression and the climate crisis through the lens of health that really helped me to understand climate justice—and eventually the excitement that comes from it.

THE STORY OF NALLELI'S PARK

A big part of climate justice is health. Creating new ways of living and new systems that ensure that all of us—especially those of us under threat—can live healthier lives. To understand some of the health impacts of the climate crisis, I'm going to introduce you to another friend: Nalleli.

Nalleli grew up in Houston, Texas. Like many kids, she loved going to play in her local park. She would always gravitate toward it—it had a great swing set, and she loved trying to swing as high as she could on it. It was a place for joy and just being a kid. **Why would a kid ever need to stop and wonder if a park was dangerous?**

When she was young, Nalleli Hidalgo never thought about whether the parks she played in were a threat. She never thought about how some of the parks were next to toxic industrial facilities. She never thought about how those plants produced fumes from burning gas, to make chemicals or other materials. Sure, like everyone, she'd heard that Houston was the energy capital of the world, producing a whopping 2.5 million barrels of oil per day. But that was always presented as a good thing, something to feel proud of. What did all that have to do with the parks that she, her friends, and her family would play in?

It was only as she grew older that she understood that the industry that produced the climate crisis had also made even going to a park damaging for kids like her.

Like for most people in the greater Houston area, seeing

long plumes of fire burning for hours and smelling **strong chemical smells from nearby industrial sites were a normal part of life.** Nalleli didn't live directly next door to an oil refinery, but sites like that were ever-present. When something is always there, you don't really notice that it may be a problem.

When she'd visit family members who lived closer to the fences that enclosed the industrial facilities, she expected that certain streets would have strong odors. But, again, this was all normal to her.

It was only through education later on that she learned how these odors would affect **the health of those who inhaled them daily.**

This knowledge came from an organization called Texas Environmental Justice Advocacy Services, also known as TEJAS, which promotes environmental protection and education. TEJAS conducts social and environmental justice tours, known as Toxic Tours, to teach people like Nalleli about environmental justice issues in the Houston area.

Environmental justice is a movement that addresses the way that marginalized communities—particularly working-class communities of color—are disproportionately harmed by hazardous waste, resource extraction, and other land uses they don't benefit from. Environmental justice promotes the fair treatment and meaningful involvement of all people, regardless of income, race, color, national origin, tribal affiliation, or disability.

The educational tours take participants through communities living in the shadow of some of the largest refineries and chemical plants, also known as *fence-line communities*. Fence-line communities bear unequal burdens, like poor air and water quality due to resource extraction from the lands surrounding toxic facilities. Through going on these tours, **Nalleli learned about the pollution these plants were releasing into the air** that she, her family members, and the whole community breathed.

She came to understand that cancer occurred at higher rates in communities closer to these plants. In particular, rates of childhood leukemia—an often-terminal form of cancer of the white blood cells—was especially high in communities on the so-called fence line. She learned that scientists believed the pollution was what was making so many people sick.

Nalleli knew people with cancer. And she worried that the toxic fumes in her community were stealing years from the lives of the people there—even from children.

It got even worse when Hurricane Harvey came.

In 2017, this hurricane flooded many homes in Texas and Louisiana, displacing families and destroying lives. The refineries and industrial sites flooded too, which prompted major malfunctions in the facilities, including chemical leaks. This released so much more pollution into the area that when residents were finally able to leave their homes they were overwhelmed by the smell of toxic chemicals.

So burning fossil fuels helped to cause intense storms like this in the first place, *and then* companies burning fossil fuels made things worse by being unprepared for these same storms and leaking more pollution everywhere.

But when things get tough, **communities have a way of coming**

together. Nalleli and other community members have repeatedly united to help respond to their community's needs. As a response to extreme weather disasters, TEJAS created a community tool-sharing program so that everyone could borrow the tools they need to recover and repair their homes. Volunteers went out to assist older people with fixing their homes. Neighbors offered their homes to shelter those whose homes were ruined.

> **When things get tough, communities have a way of coming together.**

Thanks to advocates who keep pushing forward and providing learning opportunities, Nalleli was able to go on to join TEJAS. She helps track the overall effects of pollutants in the Houston area—and campaigns for a safer environment for all. Community leaders like Nalleli have grown more determined than ever to protect our environment and our communities from the impacts of toxic pollutants.

Nalleli understands that when she sees something that moves her, she doesn't have to sit still and let it be. She has chosen time and time again to move the thing that has moved her. **It is work like Nalleli's that will transform our world**—and will ensure that no one gets left behind while we do.

The first part of Nalleli's story makes me angry and sad: No one should ever be forced to live or play somewhere that is making them sick. But in my experience, this anger is a good thing—if we channel it toward doing something about the thing that made us angry. Remember, we have to work out how to make what moves us move, or change, the world around us. That's where real hope comes from: action.

Nalleli is doing just that. Through her work, she sees people starting to fight back. They are advocating for funds that can help them prepare for and cope with extreme weather. They're taking on the fossil fuel industry for poisoning their communities. For her, the work TEJAS is doing to fight back is *health work* as much as prescribing medicine or operating on someone is.

They are going upstream. Maybe it's less flashy, but over time it will save countless lives. This is what truly matters!

IT'S BY DESIGN

Where we live around the stream matters a lot, but **sometimes it's hard to tell.** Sometimes going upstream can illuminate the fact that we've actually been living downstream: Like Tom, our health has been impacted by actions upstream! It's possible that you also live near an environmental hazard. Maybe there's an energy plant in your town. Or maybe there's a big highway that goes past your home. Or an incinerator down the road from you.

If you don't have any of these things near you, it's possible that (1) your family has enough money to choose not to live near any of these health-damaging things and/or (2) that you're white. You might be thinking that I'm making a pretty big assumption here, but it doesn't come from nowhere!

Did you know that in the United States, Black Americans over the age of sixty-four are three times more likely to die from exposure to air pollutants than white Americans? Did you also know that fossil fuel plants, incinerators, mega-highways, and other polluters are more likely to be found in communities where people of color live? And did you know that none of this is an accident? It's on purpose, *by design.* **This reality—in which Black communities in particular are exposed to more pollutants than white communities—is called *environmental racism.*** And when it comes to where people are housed, we need to talk about something called *redlining.*

To understand what redlining is and why and how it came to be, we're going to have to hop in the time machine again, to the 1930s, during the Great Depression.

The US government hopes to improve the lives of Americans with a plan called the New Deal. Part of the plan aims to make it easier for people to buy and own their own homes by making mortgages more accessible. But **the plan doesn't make these loans accessible to everyone.** In already-rich, white neighborhoods, it becomes way easier to buy a home. But neighborhoods that are poor or have high Black or immigrant populations are "redlined." This means that banks won't give loans to people in these neighborhoods because of racist ideas that they might not be able to pay them back.

For people living in these communities, **buying a home was made almost impossible.** While many white folks were able to

buy their homes and build wealth to hand down to their children, Black folks were shut out from doing the same thing. As the majority of people who lived in these poor, Black communities did not own their homes—and those who could afford to buy a home would move elsewhere—redlined areas became more and more run-down. With less wealth, these communities also had less power.

This vulnerability was capitalized on by hazardous and polluting industries who chose these areas to locate their factories—knowing they could get the land cheaper and that the nearby communities had less power to resist them.

Today, these communities have less green space access and tree cover, and have more hazardous waste facilities nearby. These communities are communities like Nalleli's. This policy of the past has meant that playing, living, and simply breathing is much safer for some kids than for others. Because actions of the past shape the present, it's important that we understand the fullness of our history while we act in the present, for the future.

Environmental racism exists all over the world. In London, a nine-year-old girl named Ella Roberta died from an asthma attack due to the air pollution in her neighborhood. Ella is believed to be the first person to have air pollution listed on her death certificate as a cause of death. She was Black and from a working-class family—both factors that increase the likelihood of living in an area with unsafe levels of air pollution.

Today, Ella's mom, Rosamund Kissi-Debrah, fights for a world where no kid will die because of the air they have to breathe. She's campaigning for clean air to be declared a human right in the UK, through a bill named Ella's Law.

Across the world, communities like Nalleli's and Rosamund's are fighting for environmental justice—so that no matter how much or how little money their family has, the color of their skin, or their background—every kid can expect not to be made sick by the neighborhood where they live.

PLAY, IMAGINATION, AND CLIMATE

While playing in the park hurt the health of Nalleli and her friends, I think play itself is essential to solving the climate crisis.

When you were younger, you probably spent a lot of time dreaming about made-up worlds. Like a world with dragons, or princesses in castles, or aliens fighting each other in spaceships, or animals talking or singing, or superheroes who can fly or move things with their mind.

If you can imagine all that . . . then you can imagine a world better than the one we live in now. In fact, kids are better at imagining new worlds than pretty much anyone else!

Every day hanging out with your friends or by yourself in your bedroom, you are creating new worlds in your mind. These are skills—superpowers, even!—that are

Kids are better at imagining new worlds than pretty much anyone else!

essential to tackling the climate crisis and building a better world for all of us. Your imagination—and your joy—is essential for us all.

Doing activism—doing work that challenges the current world and chooses to build a better one—doesn't have to be dull or boring. **It doesn't have to *feel* like work.** To choose to act comes from the purest, most excited, and most joyful part of your soul. It comes from its depth. A depth that is crying out to be seen, to be used, to transform.

That power is in all of us. Some of us may have to reach farther than others to find it, but it is there. Use it. Hold on to it. Do not let it go!

Now feels like a good place for us to do another imagining exercise. We understand the problems more clearly than we did the first time we did it, so the solutions should also be clearer. So draw out on a new piece of paper what your community would look like when we have won the fight against fossil fuels, against exploitation, against capitalism, and for a world where we all live in dignity. Again, imagine not only what it looks like but what it feels like and maybe even what it smells like!

I want you to feel like you're in this place. How different is it from the first world you imagined? Has it already expanded? Does it already feel bigger than it did before?

Now, I know we have felt a lot of things as we have gone on this journey together so far—from heartbreak to curiosity to anxiety. But for the final part of this book, I want to focus on feeling excited. Remember, **this is an *opportunity* for a better world for us all.**

We're going to feel so ecstatic for this better world that we won't be able to stop ourselves from doing the work to make it real. We are going to feel our hearts race and feel so big that they might burst from our chests. We are going to feel the joy we will feel when we achieve it. We are going to anchor our soul in this new and better world. Because we will achieve it together. Now let's work out how we can get there.

POETRY BREAK

Time for another poem! When we are imagining big, when we are expanding upon what others are telling us is possible, we might get some people telling us that we are too idealistic or that we're naive. I've heard this a lot! But I think what some people tell you is idealism or naivety is actually your biggest strength. You see the world clearly—you see the things that don't make sense that others have just accepted over time, and you see how much we could change and transform everything for the better. Keep dreaming.

POSSIBLE

I'm constantly dreaming of building a new world
I've been told that I'm
idealistic
my head is in the clouds
But really
my feet are rooted in the soil
They feel
they see how nature transforms
and so can
everything

My eyes look down on the page
and race to
absorb the words
of the ancestors who came
before us
to know that they dreamed too
to know that they built too
to learn from how they thought

My fingers rush over a keyboard
to find the best way to
excite people
to make them imagine
beyond the boundaries of
what they think is
possible

What is possible *if not the conclusion of the story*
we are all writing with our lives?

PART 3

14

COMMON GROUND BECOMES COMMON SENSE

When I was a kid, my mom used to say things like "Mikaela, make sure you always wear your seat belt!" and "Always brush your teeth before bed!" and "Always tie your laces!"

"But whyyyy?" I would say, probably whining.

"It's just common sense!" she would say.

Moms love to say something is common sense, don't they? But it's a really good way to understand a common practice, or something we all accept as reasonable, like wearing seat belts, tying our laces, and brushing our teeth.

In a more universal way, **the ideas we accept as normal or reasonable change all the time.** Did you know that a couple hundred years ago, women were not allowed to vote in national elections anywhere? Or that it was not until 1974 that women were legally allowed to have a credit card in their own name in the United States? Did you know that mere decades ago, the color of your skin determined whether or not you were allowed to swim in certain swimming pools, go into certain restaurants, attend certain schools, drink from certain water fountains, and sit in certain seats on a bus?

Lots of things that most people now would find ridiculous used to be accepted as "common sense." But over time, because of people asking questions, proposing ideas, and acting in different ways, ideas taken for granted as "just the way things are" change.

It's easy to think these big changes happen by themselves. That things simply get better over time. It's comforting to think things will take care of themselves if we sit back and let them. Wouldn't that be great?

Lots of things that most people now would find ridiculous used to be accepted as "common sense."

The reality is that things *do* tend to get better—but *only because people choose to make them better.* People work really hard sometimes for a really long time to actively shift what is seen as reasonable or normal in our world. We *actively choose* this—it doesn't magically happen to us. Intention and action is what makes the world improve. Not fate. The fact that women can vote, the fact that we have seat belts to protect ourselves from accidents, the fact that we have a "weekend" to rest from work . . . these are all things that happened because people made them happen!

A funny thing about change is that it is not the world's default setting. The default setting is inertia, or "Things are fine—there's no need to change." The same way a soccer ball won't move by itself unless you kick it, **the world won't change unless you kick it too.**

Of course, change also works in the other direction. It's possible you go to a school that bans certain kinds of books or limits how free kids are to express their gender identity. Change might be constant, but the nature of that change—whether it's good change or bad change—is not certain: That part is up to us.

There's a term for the shifting back-and-forth of what is generally accepted, or what most people consider to be common sense. **It's called the *Overton window.***

The Overton window is a tool for identifying ideas a majority of people find sensible, popular, or acceptable. Think of it like a vibe check, but for a whole country or the whole world. Governments, politicians, and activists all use it to measure the possibility for change at a moment in time on an issue. Would people find it unthinkable? Radical? Maybe popular? For any given issue, the closer the Overton window gets to the middle, the more likely a government will have the opportunity to change laws or change policy about it.

For example, the election of Donald Trump as US president shifted the Overton window away from the climate policies the

UNTHINKABLE
RADICAL
ACCEPTABLE
SENSIBLE
POPULAR
POLICY
POPULAR
SENSIBLE
ACCEPTABLE
RADICAL
UNTHINKABLE

The Overton Window is a sliding scale used to define how a population feels about an idea. For example, long ago, the idea of women voting in the United States was "unthinkable." Today, it is "policy."

world so desperately needs. "It's fake," he'd say about climate change, or "It's China's fault," and on and on he would go, until more and more people started believing him.

But it's not just presidents who have the power to move the window. **Anyone can.** Like me, for example!

When I was in university, studying to be a doctor, I became super-passionate about tackling the climate crisis. This passion brought me to a meeting for a group called Extinction Rebellion Scotland. I walked tentatively into a room filled with people I did not know. I had gone to the meeting alone, and I was nervous. After a couple minutes, a kind person named Alex came up to me from across the room and offered to talk me through what was going on.

When I left the meeting, I felt energized: I no longer had to sit and see the climate crisis unfold. I could do something about it.

The "something" we were planning was a two-week-long occupation of the roads outside Westminster Abbey and a government agency at the time called the Department for Business, Energy & Industrial Strategy, or BEIS. That's a long name for a department, but all you need to know is that **words like *business* and *industrial strategy* aren't great for the climate.**

BEIS housed both the government departments tackling the climate crisis and the department supporting the oil and gas industry. It was as if the tobacco industry and the lung doctors shared an office space. How strange!

We were targeting this area for a specific reason: to call out the UK government's support for the fossil fuel industry. Our protest site was focusing on fossil fuel subsidies (money the government pays to fossil fuel companies) in particular, but we weren't the only protest site. All across London, other groups were occupying roads and disrupting "business as usual" to bring attention to the government's outrageous climate policy. **Our overall demands were clear:** for the UK government to tell the truth about the scale of this crisis and declare a climate emergency, to organize a citizens' assembly, and to commit to drastically reducing emissions by 2025. In other words, we wanted the government to create a space for citizens to practically shape and direct policy, and to promise to reduce emissions in line with safe levels as advised by climate science.

Before these protests, many people called our demands completely unrealistic. But our job as activists is to work with others to make the "unrealistic" realistic. To make the "radical" common sense.

> Our job as activists is to work with others to make the "unrealistic" realistic.

At our site, we chatted about fossil fuel subsidies with both politicians and ordinary citizens who passed by, we did interviews, we hosted speeches and workshops, we blocked the entrances to BEIS to keep it from continuing as usual, and we stayed put, camping in the middle of the road, for almost a week. Alex and I worked together to communicate about all of this on social media too. Everything we did—everything we achieved—was only possible thanks to a huge group of people doing the work together, and through every single person recognizing that **they had an active role to play in shaping and creating change.**

It was one of the most energizing and exciting times of my life. Yes, my heart was broken by the reason we were there. But *taking action* not only put my heart back together but made it even bigger!

And after the concerted actions of many people—including me—the UK government declared a climate emergency and,

later, agreed to host citizens' assemblies. By being annoying, we had managed to force through change and make possible what was once seen as impossible. We had shifted the Overton window!

For changes like this, you need two things. First, **you need to tell better stories** so people can envision change and embrace its possibilities. But **you also need to get in the world's face sometimes.** To give people a nudge or even shake them awake.

A few years ago, my friends and I shook some more people awake at TED's climate conference in Edinburgh, Scotland. You may or may not have heard of TED talks, but they're a pretty big deal. Millions of people watch them online and many great speakers have shared their ideas. But at its first climate-focused event, TED decided to put the CEO of Shell—Ben van Beurden—on a panel about tackling the climate crisis. Yes, you read that right. . . . The same Shell that is on the list of twenty companies responsible for more than a third of greenhouse gas emissions, continues to pollute the Niger Delta, makes billions of dollars in profits every year by making the climate crisis worse, and spent over 100 million dollars in 2019 alone on greenwashing and delaying climate policy. How on earth could a fossil fuel company executive be featured at a climate conference?

You may have guessed it already, but **it was because of their social license.** This license distracts people from the reality: that fossil fuel companies do not care one bit about protecting people or our planet. They care about one thing and one thing only: making as much profit as possible for their shareholders.

When I met with the organizers to challenge them on this before the conference began, they said that Shell *needed* to be part of the conversations there. But the panel Shell's CEO was set to be on came at the same time Shell was attempting to approve drilling at the massive new Cambo oil field in the nearby North Sea. My fellow activists and I were super-angry about Ben van Beurden being given space to greenwash Shell.

At first, we tried asking nicely for the organizers to remove him from the panel. We presented them with information about the harms Shell has caused, how the company only ever blocks climate progress, and the dangers of greenwashing. **We showed them how many people agreed with us.**

Still, they refused to remove Van Beurden from the program. So I asked them to add a local climate justice activist to the panel—Lauren MacDonald, a member of the Stop Cambo campaign—who could challenge him.

The organizers agreed to this.

After lots of work behind the scenes to prepare, Lauren took to the stage, face to face with Ben van Beurden, and delivered a speech that **still brings me to tears today.**

Here are a few excerpts:

> Mr. Van Beurden, I just want to start by saying that you should be absolutely ashamed of yourself for the devastation that you have caused to communities all over the world.
>
> Every single day that you fail to stop

making evil decisions is a day that the death toll of the climate crisis rises.

Shell has spent millions covering up the warnings from climate scientists and bribing politicians.

Lauren then asked him a yes-or-no question about whether Shell would continue to block climate progress, but Van Beurden tried to get out of it without saying either of those words.

Lauren closed by saying: "I hope that you know that we will never forget what you have done, and what Shell has done. I hope you know that as the climate crisis gets more and more deadly, you will be to blame. And I will not be sharing this podium with you anymore. . . . I do not agree with Shell being given this platform."

Several activists then walked out from the auditorium, chanting "Don't just watch us. Join us."

I wasn't there in person, but I watched Lauren's speech via livestream, and it was one of the most moving things I've ever seen. I am so ridiculously proud of everyone involved—but especially Lauren, for having the bravery to challenge Van Beurden live onstage on such short notice.

Shell dropped its investment in the Cambo oil field a couple months later. **And resistance by climate activists clearly played a major part.** We can create so much change when we choose to stand up together. When we stand up, when we get in people's faces, when we stop just asking nicely.

We still have a long way to go. We need most people to think it's common sense that there should be no more fossil fuels. We need it to be common sense that reparations are essential in order to create a world where we have addressed the harms of colonialism. And we need it to be common sense that wealth should be shared in a way that **allows every single person to live a dignified and safe life.**

> **We can create so much change when we choose to stand up together.**

Now let's think about what each of us can do to start shifting the Overton window. Take "There should be no more fossil fuels" as an example. What are things you could do to make people see that this is just common sense?

I'll get things started.

You could talk about it to the people around you. Talk to the principal of your school. Ask your principal and teachers to sign a public pledge that says they're in support of your goal. Ask all your fellow students to sign a pledge too. You could campaign to show why this change is important.

To write a pledge, take out a piece of paper. **Begin your pledge with words like** "We, the students of [write the name of your school] demand an end to fossil fuels. We ask that [write the name of your principal] join us in urging [write the name of a state or local government official] to sign the Fossil Fuel Non-Proliferation Treaty, calling for no new fossil fuel projects." That's a start! It would be even better if you added in the particular reasons why you and your friends or fellow students care. The more personal, the more persuasive, the better!

Now take some time here and think about what other things you could do in your life to be part of shifting the Overton window.

If you've already written to your principal, could you write directly to a government official too? **Could you organize all your classmates to do the same?** Perhaps you could create some posters that show the reality of the fossil fuel industry and stick them up in your local area. In some cities and towns, events and even museum exhibitions are sponsored by fossil fuel companies. Could you organize with other kids and their parents to go together to protest outside these events?

When I was at school and became very passionate about veganism, I would give talks in school assemblies about the issue, invite classmates to showings of documentaries that had changed my mind about the issue, and write social media posts to raise awareness of the issue with my friends and family.

My biggest advice here would be to really try to get other people on board with you. The best way to do that is to ask your friends, your classmates, your family, and your neighbors—or whoever it is you want to join you—what do they already care about? Once you know what they already care about, you can work out how what they already care about connects to the climate crisis.

Perhaps what they care about is animals, maybe their pet. If so, you could tell them all the ways animals are being affected by the climate crisis. **When you're trying to convince people of things, it's often much better to use stories, rather than just statistics.** You may have noticed that I've often told stories from my life or my friends' lives. Stories are far more moving and interesting than numbers!

By reaching people based on what they already care about, you're way more likely to get them on board! It works so much better than saying, "I care about this issue, so you have to too!" When the people we talk to are able to see *themselves* in the issues we are talking about—when they are able to connect to them *personally*—they are far more likely to engage.

Chances are that most people you know already care at least a little bit about the climate crisis. **But most people haven't made the connection yet** to how what they care about will be threatened by the climate crisis, or they don't completely understand the connection. Reaching people where they are at, using language they already understand, is the most effective way to get new people to join in taking action with you!

These are just a few ideas, but I hope they've already got your creative juices flowing and that you'll think of many more! You can add to these ideas as we go through the final part of this book. But I don't want you to only *think* about them; I want you to start *doing* these things.

Start these conversations. Bring together some friends to organize a pledge. If you're looking for more help forming your pledge, there's some great info on the website of the Fossil Fuel

Non-Proliferation Treaty Initiative (fossilfueltreaty.org), an organization that aims to get local and national governments all over the world to sign.

Give it a go today!

15

IT IS NEVER TOO LATE

Every now and then, I hear something that annoys me even more than the loudest climate denier.

It infuriates me, and I think it's the worst thing that someone can say in the face of this crisis.

It's just three words. Three simple words.

"It's too late."

It seems like there's a certain type of person who decides to say this. It's usually someone sitting comfortably at the top of those hierarchies we spoke about earlier—a wealthy, white, older person or someone else with the means to keep their loved ones safe in times of climate crisis—who decides to loudly announce that it's too late and action is futile.

But plenty of people my age, and even younger, express the

same defeatist "It's too late" attitude. In their case, I think it comes from fear. Fear of not knowing what they can do. Fear of what the action they need to take might look like. Fear of forcing themselves into the vulnerability of a fight where success is not guaranteed.

For some, **giving up is the easy choice.** For others, it is simply not a choice at all. What about my friend Kato, whose home island is sinking? Does he have the luxury to say "It's too late"? What about Nalleli? Can she afford to say "It's too late" to stop the factories in her neighborhood from poisoning the air? What about my friend Aysha, whose home and school in Bangladesh have flooded every single year since she was five years old? What about Isaiah, a friend of mine in Kenya, whose schooling was repeatedly disrupted due to long droughts? Isaiah's family's cows have nowhere to graze, his family's livelihood is dying around them, and his entire Masai community is being forced to survive on less and less food.

None of them can afford to give up. And neither can any of us.

I believe if more people realized their real power to make real change, they wouldn't think it's too late. It's why I decided to write the book you're holding. I want you to know and to believe that no one—including you—is too young or too small or too ordinary to transform the world. And it's why I spent time in this book talking about the past, and how change happened in the past. **Because a lot of this history is often hidden;** it's not widely taught. We're taught that only heroes can make huge, historic changes. We see only the "mushrooms."

Mushrooms? Well . . . have you ever been foraging? That's

160

when you go out into nature to find edible things that grow in the wild. (It's something that takes a lot of practice and knowledge, so please don't do it unless you're with someone experienced.)

If you've been out foraging, you know the euphoric feeling of finding a big mushroom. For me in the UK, the mushroom I'm always on the lookout for is called chicken of the woods, because when you cook it, it has a similar texture to chicken!

When we find a big mushroom, we may think, "Wow! That's a miracle!" and believe it sprang up from nowhere. What we can see is just the mushroom.

What we don't see are the millions of underground networks called *mycelia*—like long roots—that expanded, nourished each other, communicated with trees, and grew underground. All of

this was invisible to us, but without it the mushroom could never have risen from the ground.

Transformational changes in our world are like these mushrooms. **They seem like miracles,** but really they are only possible because of decades of unseen work—much of which did not seem like a "win" at the time—by thousands or sometimes millions of people who built the connections to make the later big wins possible. People usually give Martin Luther King Jr. a lot of credit for advancing civil rights in the United States. And he deserves credit. But civil rights never would have happened without millions of other people showing up, marching, demanding. They are also heroes. And we can become the heroes of our history too.

We can become the heroes of our history too.

Making this mycelial work visible is everything! Highlighting the work of countless people who woke up and made a choice every day to not give up, even if they wouldn't find the big mushroom during their lifetime—that is what inspires us to see change within our grasp.

It's empowering. It reminds us that whatever our role is in these movements to change the world, it is valuable, important, and worth doing. It reminds us that **it's not too late.**

In fact, **it will never be too late.** It might take a really long time: You might not see all the changes you want to in your lifetime, but that's okay. We don't do this work because we are sure that we will win *now.* We do this work because it is the right thing to do and it will make achieving the future that we all want possible for the generations who come after us.

I often think about how grateful I am for the generations who came before me, the people who kept fighting even when they didn't see all of the transformations they wanted. They kept building mycelial networks even when they didn't see big mushrooms. Without the networks they built, **I wouldn't have so many of the freedoms I have today!**

I'm especially thankful that those who came before me in the climate fight did not quit. Without generations of organizers powering through even when they couldn't stop the oil fields they were campaigning against, we wouldn't have been able to stop the Cambo oil field. **So you and I can't give up either!**

16

TURNING "ME" INTO "WE"

Can we make a promise together now? If you've hung with me all the way through this book, then I trust you, and I hope you trust me too.

Okay, the promise I'd like us both to make is that we won't expect others to come and fix everything, and instead we'll always take on our own share of the work ourselves. When we see an issue—when we feel our hearts break—we will not look away and expect someone else to be the one to tackle it. We will ask ourselves what *we* can do to be part of the change we need. We won't limit our response to "thoughts and prayers." Good intentions and prayers may be nice, but organizing and hard work are what get things done.

When our hearts break, let's keep this mantra in our heads:

"When times get tough, we don't give up. We get organized."

Can we each put a hand on our heart and make this promise together now?

I just closed my eyes and took a few breaths as I did it. Now it's your turn.

When times get tough, we don't give up. We get organized.

So where does the journey go from here?

At this point, you have some idea about key things that are helpful: working together as a team, understanding the connections between different issues, putting pressure on governments or climate-wrecking companies by annoying them or disrupting them, and more.

Kids have played a vital role in transformational changes of the past. In many movements, young people have consistently organized alongside their elders—or sometimes even taken the lead themselves.

We've gone back in time a lot during this book—perhaps more than you expected for a book about a current issue. But, once more, let's hop into Mikaela's Time Machine!

It's 1963 in Birmingham, Alabama. Racist Jim Crow laws still exist in some states in the US, meaning Black people have been given fewer rights than white people and live in segregation. Black kids are only allowed to go to Black schools—schools that get less money than white schools. Black kids can't sit and eat at certain restaurants. Black kids generally have access to less of everything.

Life is difficult and dangerous for Black kids in Alabama in 1963. They may see family members killed by racist policing (sadly, not enough has changed there), neighbors' houses bombed by white supremacists, or friends attacked by dogs or even shot at simply for protesting for equal rights—all on top of the baseline difficulty for Black people of being given access to only low-paying jobs.

Terry Collins was fifteen years old at the time, and described it like this: "People had economic concerns and the children were not subject to that. They didn't have to be concerned about their careers being ruined and all that. We had nothing to lose. Well, our lives. But our lives were terrible anyway."

To say that times were tough would be an understatement. But like so many oppressed people throughout history, **these kids didn't allow despair to get the best of them.** They saw that they, too, could be part of change. Terry and other kids came together for what became known as the Children's Crusade.

On an otherwise normal morning in May 1963, Black kids across Birmingham tuned in to their radios waiting to decipher a code. Janice Wesley Kelsey, who was sixteen that day, remembers it clearly.

"I woke up that morning with my mind on freedom. I was so excited," she said in an NPR interview on the sixtieth anniversary of the Children's Crusade. "[The DJ on the radio] was

CHILDREN MARCH IN BIRMINGHAM,
ALABAMA, IN MAY OF 1963

saying, 'We're going to have a party in the park.' I knew what that meant—Kelly Ingram Park. 'We're going to jump and shout. We're going to turn it out.' I knew what that meant—we were going to school, but we weren't going to stay."

It wasn't just Terry and Janice. More than 1,000 Black children from the ages of seven to eighteen walked out of school that day and marched toward City Hall to call for an end to segregation. You can probably tell that this wasn't spontaneous: It was organized and planned.

For weeks before the action, the kids had been running and attending their own classes, where they learned about inequality, the systems that were creating the conditions they were being forced to live in, and the importance of taking action to make things fairer and safer. These classes helped turn general feelings that something was wrong into a drive to transform these conditions: **to refuse to accept them.**

They ran other classes that rehearsed the aggression they expected to face from police and passers-by alike. These rehearsals helped to work out who would be best on the front lines of the march and who was best placed behind the scenes.

There was a role for everybody—whether making signs, bringing food and water, running the training sessions, writing the coded instructions, or marching arm in arm. Everyone was needed, and everyone was important.

All of this preparation came together on May 2. Young Black kids poured out of school, arm in arm, singing "We Shall Overcome." **Together, they marched down the streets,** where they were met with horrifying aggression from the police force. Dogs were let loose on them, fire hoses were sprayed at them, and hundreds of kids were violently arrested. And yet so many of these kids did not run away. They stood together as the dogs came. And as the pressure of the water from the fire hoses threatened to throw them down the road, they linked their arms even tighter. The bravery of these children astounds me to this day and never fails to bring tears to my eyes.

Kids rising up to challenge the world and create change is not just a thing of the past. All over the world, kids are rising up today—and they have been consistently in recent years. Kids have been part of defending their homelands for generations. In Ecuador, a group of girls who live near the Amazon rainforest—including eleven-year-old Leonela Moncayo—won a huge court case against the government for allowing fossil fuel company Texaco to routinely use flaring in their communities, spewing toxic gases into the air!

Millions of kids across the world have gone on strike from school every Friday, as part of the Fridays For Future movement, inspired by then teenager Greta Thunberg's School Strike for Climate outside of Sweden's parliament building. This youth climate movement is an historical echo of the Children's Crusade.

The bravery and power that was with these children, **you have that power too.** Maybe you don't feel it, but it's there. It's inside you somewhere, waiting to come out. Your circumstances may be different from those of the kids in Alabama that day decades ago or the kids defending their homes in the Amazon in recent years, but we can still learn from them. They took what moved them and used it to move the world. And so can you.

POLITICAL EDUCATION

So much of what I do as an activist is turning "me" into "we." I've done my job only when I've shared and amplified what I believe so that others can decide if they want to believe it too. The only reason I write and speak about climate justice and activism is with **the hope that others will be encouraged to join and do this work too!**

At events, I get told over and over that I'm "inspiring"—at first, it was nice, but now I find it frustrating. Sometimes what people mean by this is "Thank goodness you're doing this work so I don't have to." That's not the response I want! I don't want to be called inspiring unless that inspiration is practical. I want people to work alongside me, not just cheer from the sidelines. All of us need to realize that change is a collective process: It's the result of the actions of many people, not a few heroes. Understanding this, learning how change really happens, is so important.

Learning how change really happens is so important.

The classes those kids in Alabama ran to help inform others were as important as the march itself.

If we are going to change the world, we have to know why. This knowledge of why we are fighting for the changes we need is called *political education*.

And guess what? By reading this book, you are participating in political education already!

How will you turn your "me" into "we"? Could you give a presentation to your class? Could you start a reading group for other kids where you discuss different chapters of this book or other ideas together?

If we want to multiply our impact, few things are more powerful than working with other people.

Say you have a group of people you've brought together around an issue you all care about. Let's use our earlier example of wanting to stop all new fossil fuel projects.

First, you need to map out all the *actors* (the businesses, institutions, politicians, government groups, banks, PR firms, etc.) who have power over this. Perhaps they have the power to reject new projects or create policies that could stop them, or perhaps they help companies do greenwashing or they fund and pay for these projects. **Work out as much of this as you can**—and keep mapping it.

Then be strategic. You'll want to think about which of these players your activist group is best positioned to confront. To use an example we've looked at already, maybe your local museum has a climate exhibition sponsored by Shell, like the one the Science Museum in London opened in 2021.

Maybe your local politician hasn't said or done much on this issue yet and you'd like to get them to.

Or maybe one of your parents or a parent of someone you know works for a company with close ties to the fossil fuel industry. **Maybe you think you could impact them.**

If you know that your big goal is to stop all new fossil fuel projects, what's a smaller goal on the way to that? Maybe if your target is a museum, your group's goal is to get the museum to drop the fossil fuel sponsorship and stop the greenwashing.

Once you know your target and your smaller goal, you can think about what would impact your target and help you pursue your goal. If we continue with the museum idea, you might want to try to get other young people and schools to refuse to go to the museum—a collective boycott—until the museum drops the sponsorship. You might want to organize protests in front of the museum as part of that.

So now you have a group, and you know your big goal, your smaller goal, and your target, and you have some ideas about actions you might take. You're next going to want to work out how to make these actions possible: In other words, **what's needed?** If you're organizing a protest, you might need people to make signs, people to speak to the crowd, people to make posters to publicize the protest, or people to offer water or snacks to protesters. Those are just some of the things you might need, and I'm sure you'll be able to think of many more!

For your action to happen, each portion of your plan needs to be someone's responsibility. So now your group can discuss and decide what each person's role will be.

With each person taking on a different role, **you can do much more than by going it alone.** And when we each work out our role—or offer ourselves up to take on responsibility—we become active members in building change. We can do so much more when we decide to turn "me" into "we."

17

WE ARE THE AX THAT BREAKS DOWN DOORS

Over and over, I've found that understanding how change happens has moved me from despair to empowerment. Often this feeling of panic—this eco-anxiety—comes from a place of feeling like there's nothing we can do. But through organizing campaigns and working with other passionate and heartbroken people, I've realized that *we are not powerless at all.*

We have so much power when we come together. **We are not stuck in our circumstances:** Every single thing in this world can change, and every single thing that we change matters. Every single fraction of a degree of warming reversed means lives saved or made safer. That matters. It will never not matter.

Every single change that has ever happened in this world has come from ordinary, heartbroken, passionate, messy, wonderful people deciding to channel all of that into action rather than giving in to despair. Passionate, ordinary, heartbroken, messy, wonderful people just like you!

By picking up this book, by reading this far, you've chosen to be active in the face of the old world ending around us. And you have chosen to understand how to build a new beginning. From the depth of my heart, thank you for that. I'm so grateful to be in this movement with you.

Hope is a funny thing. It's often described as something people can give you, something to be passed around. But in my life, I've found that hope is actually something we create. Hope is active. Hope is alive—but only if we organize to keep it that way.

> **Hope is active. Hope is alive— but only if we organize to keep it that way.**

My favorite way to describe hope is adapted from American writer Rebecca Solnit's book *Hope in the Dark:*

"Hope is not a lottery ticket you can sit on the sofa and clutch, feeling lucky. **It's an ax you break down doors with in an emergency.** Hope should shove you out the door, because it will take everything you have to steer the future away from endless war, from the annihilation of the earth's treasures and the grinding down of the poor and marginal. . . . To hope is to give yourself to the future—and that is what makes the present inhabitable."

This was part of a speech I gave to 30,000 people at the COP26 Climate March—organized in part by kids from the Fridays For Future movement. After I read what Rebecca Solnit had to say, I said: "We are that ax. We will break down these doors, and we must."

Together, we *are* the ax that breaks down doors. Together, we *are* the new world that breathes. Together, we *will* build a new world, because we simply have no other reasonable choice!

To be this ax, to build this hope, it helps to be rooted in a consistent role. While you can take on responsibility and smaller roles in specific campaigns, knowing your more rooted role in a movement for transformation can be grounding. Ayana Elizabeth Johnson, marine biologist and author of *All We Can Save,* has a handy Venn diagram that can help with that. It looks like this:

Find the overlap between what brings you joy, what you're good at, and what work needs doing. It's at this intersection that

you'll find a role that you'll be able to do for a long time. Not only because you're good at it, so it comes easier to you, but also because you'll enjoy the work. Joy can be an antidote to burnout! Don't leave it behind as you go on your activism journey. Joy is sustainable. Joy is essential. Joy is how we make the transformation we want to make attractive. More people will want to join us if we're enjoying the work we do!

Wow, we have been on a *journey* together! And guess what? **This is *just the start*.** Just the start of all we can know about the world we are inheriting; just the start of how much better this world can be; just the start of your activism to helping transform the world to be safer, better, and more joyful for every one of us.

I'd like us to make another promise together. Now that you'll be off doing this work, changing our world and tackling the climate crisis, can we promise that we won't leave anyone behind? That we will always be working toward a world that is big enough for everyone. Where no one is "sacrificed" for profit, where no one is forced to live next to deadly pollution, where everyone is safe. That we won't just paint the world green to make it look better: We will fundamentally and materially transform it.

I have my hand on my heart again. I'm taking a deep breath. Together, we are promising to tackle the climate crisis in a way that also tackles oppressive systems. Together, we are promising to create the world that our collective imagination deserves.

You have a whole life ahead of you that will be filled with change. That might sound scary! But that's one of the only things we can really be sure of. We could try to run away, but we would never escape this change: We'd just be ignorant of the reality. I'd rather face it head on, with you, arms linked, like the kids in the Children's Crusade.

What is exciting is that we can also be sure of the power we have to direct that change—if we choose not to look away and instead to ask, "What can I do?"

So now that we're at the end of this beginning, what are you going to do? **How are you going to make what moves you move the world around you?**

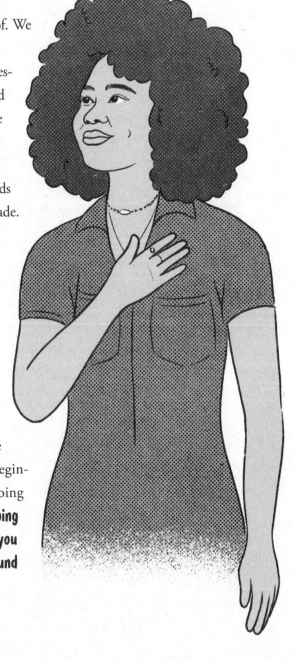

GLOSSARY

ACTIVISM: The practice of taking action to bring about social or political change

CAPITALISM: An economic system where private individuals or groups—instead of the government or the public—own companies and business. These companies compete with other companies to earn a profit.

CARBON: An element that combines with other elements to make up a large part of all living things

CARBON CAPTURE: A technological process that some people believe can remove and store carbon dioxide emissions away from the atmosphere

CARBON DIOXIDE: (CO_2) Essential for life on Earth, but also a greenhouse gas that traps heat in the atmosphere

CARBON FOOTPRINT: The impact of each person on the climate

CARBON OFFSETS: A way to make up for your carbon emissions by paying other people to do something climate-friendly, like plant trees

CLIMATE CHANGE: Long-term shifts in the Earth's temperature and weather patterns due to human activity, chiefly burning fossil fuels

CLIMATE DELAY: A strategy used by some to slow down climate action by saying there's no need to hurry or that we can afford to wait until later

CLIMATE DENIAL: The belief that climate change is not real or is not as bad as scientists say

CLIMATE JUSTICE: An approach to climate action that prioritizes the needs and priorities of the people most affected by climate change

COLONIALISM: When one country exerts power or force to take control of land or natural resources from another country

CONSUMPTION: The act of buying or using products or natural resources

EMISSIONS: Releasing carbon dioxide into Earth's atmosphere by burning fossil fuel

ENVIRONMENTAL JUSTICE: The idea that every person has the right to live in a healthy environment

ENVIRONMENTAL RACISM: Inequality that happens when communities of color are disproportionately exposed to harmful environmental conditions where they live

EQUITY: Fairness and justice. If all people are given what they need to succeed and thrive, that is equity.

EXPLOITATION: Taking advantage of someone, or treating them unfairly in a way that benefits you

EXTRACTION: The often-destructive process of removing natural resources, like oil and gas, from the earth

FLARING: The practice of burning off extra gas during fossil fuel extraction or processing

FOSSIL FUELS: Substances like oil, coal, and gas that were formed underground over millions of years from the carbon in decomposing life forms

GLOBAL NORTH: Countries of the world where industry is bigger and people generally have more money and opportunities and better living conditions as a result of their extraction of wealth from so-called "poorer" countries through colonialism or capitalist activity

GLOBAL SOUTH: Countries of the world where people generally have less money, fewer opportunities, and worse living conditions as a result of wealth being extracted away from these lands and peoples by other so-called "richer" countries through colonialism or capitalist activity. Sometimes these countries are rich in natural resources like oil and gas.

GREENHOUSE EFFECT: A process that occurs when gases, like carbon dioxide, in Earth's atmosphere trap in heat

GREENWASHING: The act of misleading people by making false claims about climate impact, or by trying to divert attention away from activities that cause harm to the Earth and its people

HIERARCHY: Organizing people according to factors like race, wealth, power, or similar criteria

HUMAN RIGHTS: Fundamental standards for human existence, like the right to freedom, justice, clean water, food, housing, and education

INEQUITY: Injustice or unfairness, or a situation where not everyone has the same tools and opportunities to succeed

OPPRESSION: When one group uses power or force to mistreat or control another group

ORGANIZE: Bring people together to build community and take action in pursuit of a shared goal. For example, achieving access to clean drinking water for your whole community.

OVERTON WINDOW: A tool for determining and expressing how receptive the public is to an idea or policy

POLITICAL EDUCATION: The process of sharing knowledge and ideas with others, particularly around ideas for social change

PROFIT: The money a business gains when they are paid more for something than it costs them to produce it

REDLINING: A discriminatory practice where banks and money identify communities or people (usually people of color) they don't want to lend money to

REPARATIONS: Paying money to a group of people harmed by a wrong. For example, Germany paid reparations to many groups after World War II.

SOCIAL LICENSE: The general acceptance of a company's business practices. If a company has social license, then it has an unspoken permission to continue operating.

SYSTEM OF POWER: A way of determining rules, beliefs, and hierarchies. Systems of power can be used to oppress and limit freedoms.

WHITE SUPREMACY: The belief that the white race is superior to other races. White supremacy is more comprehensive than just racism, because it assigns higher values and ideals to whiteness.

RESOURCES FOR FURTHER ACTION

A big thanks to Charlotte at Parents for Future UK—and her son, Grey—for sharing some of these groups and resources for kids and parents with me!

GROUPS FOR PARENTS TO JOIN

Parents for Future US: parentsforfuture.org

Here4TheKids: here4thekids.com

Mothers Out Front: mothersoutfront.org

Mothers Rise Up US: mothersriseup.org

Extinction Rebellion Families US: extinctionrebellion.us

GROUPS FOR KIDS TO JOIN

Climate Kids: climatekids.org

Fridays for Future US: fridaysforfutureusa.org

The Sunrise Movement: sunrisemovement.org

FREE ONLINE RESOURCES FOR KIDS AND SCHOOLS

Greenpeace, Monster Education Resources Pack:
greenpeace.org.uk/resources/monster-education-resource
-pack

BBC, Our Planet Now: "How to Become a Voice for Nature":
bbc.co.uk/programmes/articles/5STsK03qtJ30tH41vsSNp5y
/how-to-become-a-voice-for-nature

Climate Action Venn Diagram: ayanaelizabeth.com/climatevenn
(Work out your role in the climate movement by making
your climate Venn diagram!)

BOOKS FOR KIDS

Global by Eoin Colfer and Andrew Donkin

Stamped (For Kids): Racism, Antiracism, and You by
Ibram X. Kendi, Jason Reynolds, and Sonja Cherry-Paul

Black and British: A Short Essential History by David Olusoga

The Hunger Games series by Suzanne Collins (You might be thinking, *What does this have to do with any of this?* Well, the Hunger Games books helped me understand capitalism, extractivism, and imperialism as a kid. If you read it with that perspective, you'll get even more out of it!)

Drawn to Change the World by Emma Reynolds

MOVIES AND TV SHOWS FOR KIDS

The Lorax

Avatar: The Last Airbender (As with the Hunger Games books, apply your understandings of colonialism and power structures to this world too!)

David Attenborough documentaries, like *Blue Planet* and *Planet Earth*

BOOKS FOR PARENTS

It's Not That Radical by Mikaela Loach

Climate Action for Busy People by Cate Mingoya-LaFortune

What White People Can Do Next by Emma Dabiri

We Will Not Cancel Us by adrienne maree brown

Vulture Capitalism by Grace Blakeley

A People's Green New Deal by Max Ajl

Hope in the Dark by Rebecca Solnit

ACKNOWLEDGMENTS

Writing this book has been a complete joy and truly one of the greatest honors of my life. Being able to wake up every morning and write about all the things I wish I'd known when I was a kid—with the knowledge that I am getting the incredible honor of being the one to introduce kids to many of these ideas—was beyond a dream come true. So many people came together to make this unreal dream possible, so it's hard to know where to begin!

Tom Russell, my wonderful editor. I do not think it would have been possible to work with a kinder, more dedicated, talented, wonderful, passionate editor on this book. I mean that with the deepest sincerity! I cannot put into words how much gratitude I have for being able to work with you. You are truly a breath of fresh air. The moment we met on Zoom, I knew that we would make a great team. (Especially when you said you wanted us to get a bunch of kids to become anti-capitalist activists!) You've approached this entire process with such grace and openness, and an essential belief that a better world *is* possible. Somehow, over and over and over, you've managed to exceed my expectations. You made this project a complete and utter joy—which is not always the case when writing books! This book is as wonderful as it is because of your energy for it. Every one of your edits or suggestions significantly improved this book. I'll never be able to say it enough, but thank you for everything.

Barbara Marcus, president and publisher of Random House Children's Books, without you none of this would have happened at all! It's not often that one can say this with complete surety, but meeting you changed my life! Again, no words can truly express how grateful I am for that and everything you've done for me, young people, and the wider climate justice movement by publishing this book. I'm so grateful for your belief in me from the very beginning and your constant generosity ever since. Thank you for every piece of advice you have offered me—and for believing in this book before it even existed! Your warmth and directness have been so valuable. I am grateful every single day that I decided to accept the invitation to speak at that conference in Finland! Thank you for championing this book and having the vision to see the transforming power it could have for young people from the very beginning.

Remember the mycelium and mushroom metaphor from the book? So much invisible underground work happens for any mushroom to fruit. Lots of that work was done by many more wonderful people—all of whom have also made this book possible and all of whom I have immense gratitude for! So much work has to be done for a book like this one to make it into your hands! So, my deepest thanks to the rest of the incredible, enthusiastic, passionate, and talented team at Random House Kids for their work on *Climate Is Just the Start:* Eugenia Lo, publishing assistant; Alison Stoltzfus, senior director of publishing; Rebecca Vitkus, managing editor; Jen Valero, designer; Alison Kolani and Maddy Stone, copy editors; and Jen Valero, book designer. I'd also like to thank Philip Pascuzzo for the incredible cover and Lauri Johnston for the other illustrations throughout the book—you really brought it to life!

Kemi Ogunsanwo, my legendary literary agent (probably the only person I'd reserve the word *legendary* for!). You have been in my corner for years now and have always believed that so much more is possible for me than I've been able to see in many moments. Thank you for believing in me from the very beginning—and always fighting for me to get what I deserve! You really are an icon! Getting to work with you is a joy and an honor. I'm excited for what we will do next!

To Nalleli, Isaiah, Ayesha, and Kato: Thank you for your generosity in sharing your stories with me and allowing me to include them in this book. Nalleli asked me to name her grandma Aleja here to honor her and her ancestors. As someone who also loves her grandma very much, I think this is so beautiful.

To my preschool teacher Miss Priestley—thank you for encouraging me to write and imagine from the moment I entered your classroom at five years old. I wrote my first book in your class—a picture book about tooth fairies—and I think that led me to where I am today. Thank you for accepting me as I am and encouraging me to be more rather than less.

To the Loach Class at London Fields Primary School—and to your amazing teacher, Jean—I am so glad you were the first group of people I told that I was writing a kids' book! I'm so excited for you all to read it.

Now I have to thank my family!

To my wonderful mum, Alcia, thank you for telling me stories of change and transformation from a young age, and not discouraging me from my activism even when it took me down paths you didn't quite expect. You have such a huge heart, and it's why mine is able to hold so much space. I learned how to be generous and kind from you first.

To my lovely dad, Mark, thank you for encouraging me to ask "Why?" and "What are you going to do about it?" ever since I was a kid. As an adult, thanks for encouraging me to follow my passions and my heart. I'm so grateful for your support in me living a life that brings me the most purpose and joy!

To my little (well, not so little now) brother, Josh, thank you for believing in me more than anyone else for as long as I can remember. You were able to see that the work I am doing and the life I live is where I was meant to be far before I or anyone else could. Thank you for loving me, for supporting me, and for telling me how proud you are of me. I'm lucky to have a brother as wonderful as you.

To my grandma, uncles, aunts, and cousins in Jamaica: I do so much of this work for you. I love you all.

To my T, my partner in life. Loving you—and being loved by you—is my favorite thing about being alive. I truly could not ask for a more supportive partner. Thank you for challenging me, for always giving me advice, for laughing and dancing in the kitchen with me, and for coming to (almost) every single event I do. I love you with every part of my soul. We are so lucky to have found each other in this life!

To my niece Sophie. You were the first person who got to read bits of *Climate Is Just the Start,* and I kept in Kato's "Funny" game for you! Your feedback was so useful! You are such a smart, caring, kind, bubbly person, and I'm so proud to be your auntie!

To my bestie, Rhiannon. Thank you for always picking up the phone, for encouraging and loving me every day. It's an honor to struggle and organize alongside you, compa.

To Momo, Bibi, Neil, Disha, Adri, Nat, Mitzi, Sherlyn, and Jess: the pals who have encouraged me so much during this whole writing process. I love you all dearly.

Finally, to you, the reader! Thank you for trusting me with your time. Thank you for leaning into transformation. Thank you for holding on to your soft heart. I love you for that. I hope we'll meet again—whether on the streets, in your school, or in another book!

ABOUT THE AUTHOR

MIKAELA LOACH, named by *Forbes*, *BBC Women's Hour*, and *The Guardian* as one of the most influential women in the UK climate movement, is a British Jamaican former medical student, a climate justice organizer, and director of the AWETHU School of Organising. Her first book, *It's Not That Radical: Climate Action to Transform Our World*, was an instant indie bestseller. She was named the 2023 Non-Fiction Indie Champion by Bookshop.org and one of the "World's Top Thinkers" by *Prospect* Magazine. Mikaela has boldly challenged powerful entities, calling out billionaires at the Bill and Melinda Gates Foundation's annual event, taking the UK government to court in the landmark "Paid to Pollute" case in 2021, and challenging Shell's CEO and board at their annual general meeting, for their human rights abuses against the people of the Niger Delta in Nigeria.